The
Encyclopedia
of WEIRD

SHEILA DE LA ROSA

The Encyclopedia of WEIRD

Tor Kids!

A Tom Doherty Associates Book   New York

THE ENCYCLOPEDIA OF WEIRD

This book is printed on acid-free paper.

Photographer: Harrod Blank
Car Artist: Albert Guibarra
Driver: Mike Andreeha
Owner: Don Tognotti
Catsup-bottle Water Tower: C. P. Fischer Photograph

A Tor Book
Published by Tom Doherty Associates, LLC
175 Fifth Avenue
New York, NY 10010

www.tor.com

Tor® is a registered trademark of Tom Doherty Associates, LLC.

Library of Congress Cataloging-in-Publication Data

De La Rosa, Sheila.
      The Encyclopedia of weird/Sheila De La Rosa. – 3rd ed.
       p. m.
      "A Tom Doherty Associates book."
      ISBN 0-812-55536-8
      EAN 978-0812-55536-3
      1. Curiosities and wonders. I. Title
      AG243.D5   1997   96-43486
      021.02–dc20   CIP

First edition: October 1998

Printed in the United States of America

0 9 8 7 6 5 4 3

to David, for a life that makes my heart smile.

to Lucy B., for always kissing me when I pick her a bouquet.

to Miguel, for unabashedly photographing his daughters from the 50-yard line.

Contents

Acknowledgments

It takes more than one writer tapping away on her keyboard to pull off a book like this. I would like to thank especially the following invaluable people:

My editor, Jonathan Schmidt, for coming up with the vision for this project and for calibrating his Weird-O-Meter with mine.

My true-blue friend and editor Suzanne Harper, for giving me a monthly forum in *Disney Adventures* in which to let loose my latest collection of weird-yet-true gems, and for being the Voice of Reason when my weirdness runs wild.

The helpful staffs at the public and private librar-ies of Portland, where I spent many a rainy day researching the world's curiosities.

My friends and family across the country, for passing along tidbits of weirdness gleaned from the newspapers, magazines, and books that they read during the last year. Following up on these leads resulted in some of the book's best entries.

To Libby La Paz, for keeping me centered for our daily walks.

Finally, a heartfelt thanks to the many, many people who shared with me the intimate details of their weirdly wonderful lives and collections. May your enthusiasm for the unusual continue to bring you as much pleasure as you've given me.

Introduction

I *love* weird stuff! I visit weird museums. I like to read about weird people. And look at weird photographs like a turn-of-the-century picture of a train wreck that hangs in my living room. I even grow weird-colored flowers in my garden. Most people grow zinnias in eye-popping yellows, reds and hot pinks. My zinnias have flowers as green as their stems.

My Weird-O-Meter first went wild a few years ago when I was returning from the Outer Banks, that skinny strip of land off the North Carolina coast. I had to check out this story I'd heard: just 45 minutes away in the small town of Belhaven was a museum that included in its collection a couple of fleas—dead ones, of course—that were dressed up like a bride and groom! The woman flea was supposedly decked out in a teeny-tiny wedding gown; the man flea in a teeny-weeny tux! My husband David and I, always ready to brake for weirdness, knew we had to see them. We decided to spring for a motel room and see the fleas the next day.

Just after the museum opened the next morning, David and I were peering through a magnifying glass at the decked out duo. We weren't disappointed. The fleas were perfectly outfitted to walk down the aisle! I still put the Belhaven museum at the top of my all-time favorite list of museums. And not just because of the flea bride and groom. I also loved Belhaven's doll that was mounted on the head of a pin and museum's stash of 30,000 buttons.

When people found out that I was writing this book, they always wanted to know how I decided whether something was weird or not. Well, sometimes it's in the numbers. Save *one* airline-sickness bag from an overseas flight, for example, and you've got an offbeat souvenir. Collect 1,060 of them as a guy in Texas has, and your collection becomes world-class weird.

Bizarre behavior is another way to walk away with a way weird award. Take insects. Liking them is cool. *Eating* them—at least in this country—is weird. Doing something ordinary in an extraordinary place is yet another route to wackiness. It's snooze news when you grow grass on the ground, for example. Grow grass on a car, however, and you've got something strangely cool.

If you, too, have tastes that run just-this-side-of-strange, you'll love this encyclopedia's entries. You'll find weird animals like dogs that tan. Insects like man-eating ants. Wacky museums like the International Banana Club Museum. Not-to-be-missed tourist attractions like a 70-foot-tall catsup-bottle-shaped water tower that pilots use as a navigating point when they fly into the St. Louis airport. Even bizarre inventions like the Velo-Douche, a strange contraption designed to let you ride a bike and take a shower at the same time.

My personal favorites are the historical items. While

researching my book, I learned that some Civil War soldiers were not the fighting men they claimed to be. They were *women* masquerading as men! That the post office once delivered mail in parts of the Southwest *by camel*. And that in the Canary Islands, some natives "speak" Silbo, a language that is totally whistled. Who says history has to be boring?

I have heard of people who like to "make good time" when they travel. They're the ones who never ever leave the expressway to make a 30-mile detour down winding country roads to visit a monastery that has, say, a football-sized hairball in its archives. Now, in my book, *that's* weird!

Sheila De La Rosa
Portland, Oregon

Animals

ARMY ANTS. Left. Right. Left, right, left. One of the fiercest armies in Africa and South America is made up of millions of half-inch-long warriors: black ants called army ants. They terrorize villagers by eating any insect, animal, or human whose path they cross during their monthly sixteen-day march.

Marching eighteen abreast in columns that stretch back hundreds of yards, the ants use their sharp jaws to tear the flesh and limbs off their victims. Insects. Mice. Just-fed pythons. Baby animals. Elephants. People, too! Finally, a military unit with no beefs about its chow!

BASILISK LIZARD. Animals aren't supposed to be able to walk—or run—on water, but the basilisk lizard can.

When the basilisk feels threatened, it rears up on its hind legs and starts running. *Run, run, run, run, run,* it seems to tell itself. Even if it comes to a river or lake, it keeps its birdlike feet going double-time. *Run, run, run, run, run!* Thanks to its big feet and lightweight body, it can run across the water for up to a quarter of a mile!

The basilisk, native to Central America, looks a lot like an iguana. It's mostly green with a sprinkle of blue and black scales and grows about three feet long, including its tail.

Excuse me! Pardon me! Comin' through.

BLONDE MANGALITZA PIG. You might describe some-body creepy who pretends to be nice as "a wolf in sheep's clothing," but in Hungary there's a breed of pig that actually has fleece like a sheep's!

The Blonde Mangalitza is large and round and bred to be turned into lard. It's also the only pig that grows long sheeplike fleece; the only other pig that did—the Lincolnshire Curly Coat—is now extinct.

BOMBARDIER BEETLE. Don't mess around with this bug. It uses chemical warfare to defend itself!

The bombardier beetle's secret weapon lies in its tummy. Literally. It can rotate the tip of its abdomen like a garden hose nozzle, aim it at an enemy, and fire off a twenty-six-mile-per-hour spray of burning-hot poisonous chemicals! Each "shot" is actually a series of microexplosions made when two chemicals (stored in separate parts of the beetle's abdomen) combine in a special gland and cause a chemical reaction that you can actually hear! Who'd of thought some beetles could make their own mace?

For this guy, a little ZAP'll do ya!

THOMAS EISNER AND
DANIEL ANESHANSLEY,
CORNELL UNIVERSITY

Weird Recess Chatter

And that's not counting **all** the people who **bug** you. Scientists have identified one million animal species; 85 percent of them are insects.

Bone soir!

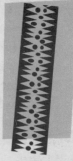

Weird Recess Chatter

Le cabbie's best friend In Paris, one in seven taxi drivers ride with canine co-pilots. The cabbies say they share the front seat with their dogs for companionship and protection.

CATAHOULA LEOPARD DOG. Meet a spotted hound dog with webbed feet and, often, *white* eyes. Say, what?

This medium-sized breed has been big in the Catahoula Lakes area of Louisiana ever since the sixteenth century, when Spanish conquerors abandoned their wounded mastiffs. The Indians didn't want to see the dogs die, so they nursed them back to health. After the mastiffs recovered, they were mated with the Indians' own dogs. ¡Caramba! The Catahoula Leopard dog was born.

"Cat" dogs are also known as "hog dogs" or "cow dogs," because they help cowboys round up pigs and cattle. Their webbed feet make them good swimmers. So what's the deal with the white eyes? Cowboys call them "glass eyes." A lot of Cat dogs also have white spots, called "glass cracks," in their brown or green eyes.

CHINESE HAIRLESS CRESTED DOG. Now *this* is a dog that's made for the shade. The reason why? Chinese Hairlesses have *no* hair and can get real bad sunburns, real quick (yeah, it tans, too!).

This breed has a small, deerlike body and usually weighs no more than twelve pounds. Its soft skin comes in blue, pink, lavender, honey, red, white, or black. And get this: they were once used as doggy heating pads! If you had an aching shoulder or a sore back in 100 B.C., your doctor might have just said, "Take one Chinese Hairless Crested and call me in the morning!" Try doing *that* with your Golden Retriever.

the Weird
list

DOGGONE WEIRD DOG PASTIMES

If you think your dog should get press coverage for its Frisbee-catching ability, think again. Here are a few hounds whose favorite ways to play catch are truly news-making material!

Name	Breed	Favorite pastime	Amazing details
Shadow	Flat coated Retriever	Scuba diving (she also water skis *and* snow skis!)	* Shadow can stay underwater for an hour in 25-foot-deep water! * her favorite diving buddy is a moray eel!
Bitsy	Yorkshire Terrier	Bicycle touring	* Bitsy has ridden 7,000 miles in a basket on the back of her owner's tandem bike!
Apache	Golden Retriever	Surfing	* Apache does 180s and 360s atop her own custom-made surfboard!

CLEANER WRASSE FISH. A trick question: How do fish that live in the ocean stay clean? ("Duhh, by constantly swimming in water?") The right answer: By getting the once-over from the Cleaner Wrasse.

Cleaner Wrasse are the housekeepers of the sea. These black-and-silver fish use their thick-lipped mouths to suck out any parasites from the mouths and gills of other fish. There are even special coral reefs—kind of like car washes for fish—where fish of many different species line up (sometimes daily!) and wait their turn for the Cleaner Wrasse to suck them clean.

The weird part is that a lot of the fish in "line" are natural enemies and usually eat each other for lunch! (Imagine standing between a grizzly bear and a python while waiting for *your* bath.) For some reason, the fish call a temporary truce until they get cleaned up. Once they're parasite-free, they go back to turning each other into the Special of the Day.

Weird Recess Chatter

Weirdest Frisbee-dog stunt. Three-time national Frisbee-dog champion Ashley Whippet is best remembered for a stunt he pulled at the 1975 Orange Bowl: the whippet leaped so high that it grabbed a Frisbee off the crossbar of the goalpost during halftime!

DOLPHIN SQUADRON. Ensign Primo? Most dolphins spend their days frolicking in the ocean. But about 100 Atlantic Bottlenose dolphins have a pretty unusual life. They're in the navy!

Yeah, the navy. For more than twenty-five years, the navy has collected, named (Primo, Puma, Skippy), studied, and trained dolphins ("self-propelled marine vehicle" in navy-speak). The flippered fleet is based at the Naval Command, Control, and Ocean Surveillance Center in San Diego, California. They travel by C–130 cargo airlift to places like Hawaii, where the dolphins are taught to spot, mark, and retrieve objects in the ocean.

Some of the squadron has even seen war duty. In 1971, a team of dolphins went to Vietnam to guard the U.S. fleet. Sixteen years later, six dolphins went to the Persian Gulf to protect the navy's floating command post.

The navy won't say *exactly* what the dolphins are trained to do if they come across, say, enemy frogmen. But rumor has it that the dolphin patrols are trained to do everything from sounding an alarm to injecting an intruder with a carbon-dioxide-filled syringe to kill them. Now that's a Flipper with an attitude!

88 BUTTERFLY. Too bad there isn't a football team named the 88ers. If there was, it'd be easy to find their perfect team mascot: the 88 butterfly.

One of Brazil's most common butterflies has double eye spots (colorful circles on the back) so closely spaced on the underside of each hindwing that they actually form the number 88. It looks like it's wearing a teeny-tiny football jersey!

The red, black, and white butterfly is only about an inch and a half long, wing to wing. It lives in the tropical forests of South America where some forty other species share the 88 hindwing pattern.

FLASHLIGHT FISH. Wouldn't it be cool to have built-in flashlights near your eyes that would make it easier to mess around outside after dark? Flashlight fish actually have such a setup.

What looks like a flashlight below each eye of this small fish is really a bazillion glowing bacteria that lives on its skin. The fish can even close "eyelids" to keep the glow-in-the-dark bacteria from blowing its cover. Flashlight fish live in caves and go out only on pitch-black nights when they use their "flashlights" to navigate and to attract prey. They also know how to trip up any fish that might want to have Flashlight fish for dinner; they blink and then swim away double-time to confuse it!

So what's bad about being a Flashlight fish? Well, you just might get blown up for being something you're not. That really happened in 1967 during the Arab-Israel conflict. A bunch of Flashlight fish were swimming in the Gulf of Eilat, their lights blinking on and off about seventy-five times a minute. *Over there! Enemy frogmen!* thought some military person. *Ka-boom!* An entire school of flashlight fish was blown to smithereens

FRINGE-LIPPED BAT. *"Bat, come! Bat, stay! Bat, fly to the right!"* Sound far-fetched to think you can teach an old bat new tricks?

Believe it or not, this species of bat has learned verbal and hand signals in as little as two hours! The fringe-lipped bat has a three-and-a-half-inch-wide body and lives in parts of Mexico, Peru, and Brazil. *"Bat, do my chores!"*

Bat's incredible!

MERLIN D. TUTTLE, BAT CONSERVATION INTERNATIONAL

GECKO. Startle a gecko and it just might do something really weird, like leave behind its tail!

Seriously. A gecko can voluntarily shed its tail (scientists call it "tail autotomy"). It leaves it behind as a decoy to occupy whatever's chasing it while the gecko escapes to safety. Not to worry, though. The tail grows back. The new tail may be shorter and have less grip than the original, but that's a small price to pay for keeping the lizard from becoming a main course.

Geckos originated in Southeast Asia about fifty million years ago; there are 800 species today. Most are about ten inches long. They are covered in small, flat scales that are green, brown, gray, blue, or yellow.

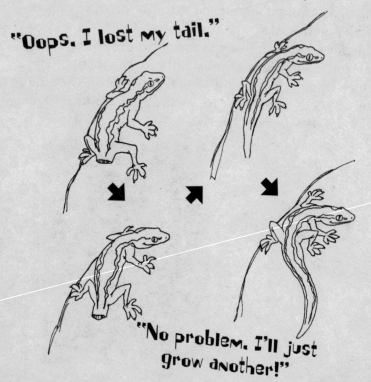

"Oops. I lost my tail."

"No problem. I'll just grow another!"

GOLDEN ZEBRA. If you ever see this zebra on TV, don't assume the color's out on the tube. Unlike the black-and-white stripes that most zebras share, the Golden zebra is brown with black zebralike markings on its legs and haunches.

The offspring of a pinto horse mom and a zebra dad, Golden zebras are extremely rare. They take after zebras in that they don't lie down, and they don't attract flies. But when it comes to food, the Golden zebra eats like, well, a horse! One 400-pound yearling eats about twenty-five pounds of hay a day.

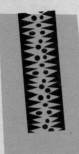
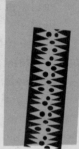

Weird Recess Chatter

"Hello, **Muffin?** Does my witty-**bitty** kitty cat miss **Mommy?"** Thirty percent of pet owners, when they're out of town, "talk" to their pets on the phone or leave them a message on the answering machine.

MUNCHKIN CAT. A Munchkin that would have felt out of place in *The Wizard of Oz*? No way, you say? Well, this Munchkin would have because it's...a cat!

All of the 300 Munchkins that exist today are descendants of one short-legged stray found under a pickup truck in Rayville, Louisiana, just twelve years ago. Their bodies are full-sized, but their front legs are only about three inches tall (the back legs measure in at around four inches). That's about half as long as the average cat's. When these dachshunds of the cat world are standing, they look like they're sitting. When Munchkins walk, they look like they're walking downhill.

If you decide you want a Munchkin for a pet, start stockpiling your allowance now. The cats cost as much as $1,500 each—cat food and rubber mouse not included!

This cat's So small, it only has eight lives.

NARWHAL. Now here's a whale only a dentist could love. Male narwhals—fifteen-foot-long whales—have an eight-foot-long, tusklike front tooth that grows in a spiraled point through its gum and out its lip.

These dark gray unicorns of the sea don't use their tusks to kill prey; they usually feed on cod, shrimp, and squid. They use their tusks as a weapon, thrusting the swordlike tusk as far as two feet into another whale!

Narwhals live in arctic waters between Greenland and Canada. In fact, Greenlanders eat narwhal meat. Narwhal burger, anyone?

This whale's got a built-in pool cue.

NORWEGIAN PUFFIN DOG. As far back as the 1500s Norwegian farmers got tired of scrambling up and down rugged cliffs above the sea hunting seabirds called puffins. Then they got a brainstorm! Hey, they'd breed the perfect dog to do it for them.

What they dreamed up is *this* foxlike breed, also known as the Lundehund (*lunde* is the Norwegian word for puffin). The dog, usually weighing no more than fifteen pounds, has *six* toes per paw, which let it speed up cliffs at breakneck speeds. It has an owllike neck that swivels around so far that its nose can touch its spine, allowing it to turn around in the narrowest of cracks where the puffins lay their eggs. It even has closeable eardrums so that it can keep them free of dirt, snow, and water when it chases puffins into mountain caves. Is this the perfect puffin terminator or what?

Weird Recess Chatter

Weird **White House pets.** President Calvin Coolidge kept a pet raccoon named Rebecca; President Woodrow Wilson had a tobacco-chewing ram named Old Ike; and President Theodore Roosevelt had a six-toed cat!

OLD RIP, THE EMBALMED TOAD. Talk about a tough day at the office! Old Rip, a horned toad, was hanging out at the Eastland, Texas, courthouse in 1897 when he accidentally got sealed into the cornerstone of the building. Nobody knew what happened until thirty-one years later, when the courthouse was demolished and the cornerstone was opened. The weird part was, Old Rip was still alive! Because of his near-death experience, he became a superstar. In fact, when he finally went to the Big Pond in the Sky, his body was embalmed and laid to eternal rest in a tiny open casket in the new courthouse. Way to go, *RIP!*

PERUVIAN INCA ORCHID DOG. Got a teacher whose face turns red when he gets upset? That's just what happens when the Peruvian Inca Orchid dog gets wound up.

The breed dates to the thirteenth century, when Indians in Peru used the dogs to warm up their beds before they turned in for the night. They were also used for hunting. The pink- or white-skinned dogs were usually kept in rooms decorated with orchids, which explains another part of their name.

POISON ARROW FROG. If Rambo had a frog for a sidekick, this would be the frog. The Poison Arrow frog is green with black dots and smears that make it look like it's camouflaged for war. It also comes with ammo: its skin!

RAY COLEMAN, PHOTO RESEARCHERS, INC.

Here's the deal. Its skin contains a poison which paralyzes the heart and nervous system. The Indians of Central and South America used to drive a stick through the Poison Arrow frog and roast it marshmallow-style until the poison dripped out (one frog has enough poison for forty darts). They'd dip their arrowheads in the poison, then head for the jungle to hunt. Who needs a gun when you've got this frog around?

SAW-SCALED VIPER SNAKE. If snakes had theme songs, the saw-scaled viper's would be "Mr. Sandman." It likes to bury itself in sand with only its yellow eyes exposed! When someone unknowingly walks near it, *fvvvvitz!,* it springs from the sand and shoots its deadly venom into the veins of the unsuspecting.

Named for the pointed tips of its brown-and-tan scales, the saw-scaled viper likes to hang out with thousands of its own kind. But don't let the fear of being watched by all those teeny-weeny eyes keep you off your favorite beach just yet. The saw-scaled viper is only found in Eastern Africa, Egypt, the Middle East, and India. *Whew!*

SCOTTISH FOLD CAT. Most cats have perky, pointed ears atop their head. The Scottish Fold has ears as deflated as two flat tires.

Scottish Folds were first discovered in—where else—Scotland in 1951. They have a round head, full cheeks, a short, thick neck, and short, sturdy legs. They can have short hair or long hair, and be black and white or calico, but they all have little collapsed ears.

SEA CUCUMBER. Don't mess around with this mellow-sounding creature. It just might hit you with its best shot: its intestines.

Sea cucumbers look like overgrown, wart-coverd-worms. They come in a lot of differentsizes, colors, and shapes. The number of retractable, armlike tentacles each species has, for example, varies from five to thirty! But it's how the animal protects itself that attracts attention.

Here's how the sea cuke's weird self-defense system works. When the marine animal is attacked, it shoots its digestive organs (picture tangles of white, sticky string) out of its butt to startle and entangle its enemy. But the sea cucumber's secret weapon doesn't protect it from everyone. In China, people love to eat dried sea-cuke (they call them *trepang*) soup. *Mmmm, mmmm, good!*

SEA HORSE. Call them Mr. Moms.

In the underwater world of the sea horse, the *males* are the ones who incubate the eggs and give birth.

These cute marine fish with the horselike heads, plated bodies, and long tails live in grass beds or floating seaweed patches. They've been known since about 50 A.D.

THAI RIDGEBACK DOG.
Everybody has a bad hair day once in a while, but this dog is actually named for its major cowlick problem.

Native to Thailand (there are only about fifty in the United States), the Thai Ridgeback has a pretty normal-looking coat of hair for a dog, with one exception. For some weird reason, the hair along the ridge of its back grows in the opposite direction from the rest of the dog's coat. The result? A short, Mohawklike ridge only its owner could love. So far, Thai Ridgeback lovers aren't turning their backs to this breed. They're shelling out as much as $1,500 for a Thai puppy.

TURKEY VULTURE. Here's a bird that makes a real pig of itself—in more ways than one.

First off, turkey vultures love meat, but they don't like to kill, so they pig out on roadkills like splatted squirrels, raccoons, and possums. Their souped-up digestive system nukes the dangerous germs that thrive on the mowed-down animals.

That said, don't stick around when another animal confronts it. That's when the turkey vulture unleashes its secret weapon: vomit. It barfs all over its attacker!

Worse, yet, when the weather gets too hot, the turkey vulture has a most unsocial way of keeping cool. It pees on its own legs!

Roadkill Recipe:

Tasty Pounded Possum

INGREDIENTS: One Possum Lightly Mashed (a station wagon–flattened possum if available)

DIRECTIONS: Season possum, fry on blacktop, and serve immediately with

vulture vomit.

Serves six

Weird Recess Chatter

Cowabunga!

Farmers in Beverly, England, dress their cows in white and yellow leggings. No, they're not hard up for a date! They're just trying to make their moosters more visible to car drivers, who have killed more than forty cows in two years. The leggings reflect light when headlights are shined on them.

VAMPIRE MOTH. Not all bloodsucking vampires are the red-caped kind you see in the horror movies. Meet one that's a moth.

The khaki-colored vampire moth has a barbed tongue that lets it cut through an animal's hide and feed on its blood. Elephants, cattle, and deer are among the mammals it likes to suck on at night. This little bloodsucker (its wingspan is only an inch and a half wide) lives in the tropical forests of India, Sri Lanka, and Malaysia.

ZEBRA BUTTERFLY. A butterfly with BO? You betcha. The Zebra butterfly is so stinky that most birds leave it alone.

Found mainly in the tropical forests of Central and South America, Zebra butterflies are black with pale yellow and white zebralike bands. It has a wingspan of three inches.

Weird Recess Chatter

Way-l o n g
worm. The longest worm in the world is the *Linnaeus longinus*, which measures as long as 180 feet long when full-grown.

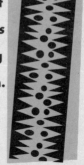

Places

BELHAVEN MEMORIAL MUSEUM, BELHAVEN, NORTH CAROLINA. Look through a magnifying glass in this museum and a pair of dead fleas decked out in wedding clothes will stare back at you. Seriously! The "groom" wears a tux, the "bride," a wedding gown. Then look around at all the other stuff that makes this place the best pack-rat palace in the country.

The museum is a monument to Eva Way, a Belhaven woman who used to raise money for the Red Cross by letting people come through her house and see all the weird stuff she collected. How weird? Well, try a doll mounted on the head of a pin. Or jars and jars of mutant animals preserved in formaldehyde, like an eight-legged pig and a two-headed fawn. One East Coast museum even heard that a sailor had sent Way a tusk from an ancient mammothlike animal. Would Eva donate it to the museum, they asked? "No way!" was Way's response.

When Way died in 1962, she was a local legend. Her hometown decided her 500,000-piece collection was too cool to let go and the Belhaven Memorial Museum was set up in the second floor of the town's city hall. More than 5,000 people a year traipse through the museum to see Way's way-cool finds.

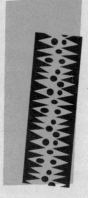

Weird Recess Chatter

"Now that's what I call a car dent!" A plaster replica of the world's largest hailstone is on display at the Dalton Museum in Coffeyville, Kansas. It's the size of a grapefruit!

CARHENGE, ALLIANCE, NEBRASKA. You don't have to cross the Atlantic to experience the grandeur of Stonehenge, the famous prehistoric monument in England. Head for the Great Plains instead.

There, in the western part of Nebraska, you'll come upon Carhenge, an all-auto replica of its overseas namesake. A Nebraskan who had spent time in England spent eight days and $12,000 to install Carhenge at his family reunion in 1987. Instead of a circle of giant boulders, thirty-two upright Fords, Chevys, and Caddies—all spray-painted gray—form a 96-foot-wide circle. Tourists from all over the world have stopped to see the 128-wheel attraction. The summer solstice is celebrated there annually with a big picnic.

CATSUP-BOTTLE WATER TOWER, COLLINSVILLE, ILLINOIS. Not to squeeze it on a little thick, but this landmark is the world's biggest bottle of catsup.

The condiment container in question? A seventy-foot-tall replica of a Brooks Old-Fashioned Catsup bottle that stands atop a 100-foot-tall tower in Collinsville, Illinois, about ten miles east of St. Louis. The catsup-red bottle with a red, white, and blue label was designed to hold 100,000 gallons of water when it was built in 1949. (There's no water stored in it right now.) At the time, Collinsville was the headquarters of Brooks Foods, a catsup manufacturer, which relocated to Indiana in 1963.

The catsup bottle looms so large that you can see it from three miles away, even farther if you're in the air. At nearby St. Louis's Lambert Airport, pilots arriving from the northeast use the giant condiment bottle as a sight check. When they get to Collinsville's cat-

C.P. FISCHER PHOTOGRAPH

sup bottle, pilots head due west across the Mississippi River.

In Collinsville, when someone asks you to pass the catsup, you'd better line up a construction crane!

Now if only they could build a 100-foot hamburger!

COCKROACH HALL OF FAME, PLANO, TEXAS. If you want to see miniature insect versions of some of the biggest names in Hollywood, crawl over to the Cockroach Hall of Fame in Plano, Texas.

The hall of fame is the buggin' idea of exterminator Michael Bohdan, owner of the Pest Shop. For five years, Bohdan awarded $1,000 to whoever turned in the biggest American roach of the year (a 2.08-inch roach from 1987 holds the record). He also sought out the country's best-dressed roaches. This thirty-roach collection holds the nattiest cockroaches from the 1,000 entries that Bohdan received each year.

Take Marilyn MonRoach, a roach decked out in a blond wig, a white dress, and high heels. Then there's Liberoache, a white-fur-caped roach seated at a baby grand piano complete with tiny candelabras. And Elvis Roachley (fashionably zipped up in a pint-sized sequined jumpsuit, of course!).

Roach fans from as far away as Germany have paid their respects to Plano's roach-a-rama.

MICHAEL BOHDAN

MICHAEL BOHDAN

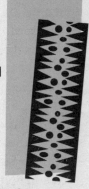

Weird Recess Chatter

The **street** name **game.**

Second Street is the most common street name in the country. You'd think it would be First Street, but a lot of streets that used to be named First Street were renamed Main Street.

FAKE STREETS. Where in the world do fake streets exist? No, not in cyberspace. Some map companies actually work in fake streets on their city and regional maps! They're not trying to trip up travelers. They're trying to nab their competitors.

Maps that show every single street in a city are really, really hard to tell apart. So how does map company A know that map company B

"Make a left at the next stop....Oops. I mean...make a right. No. A Left!"

isn't ripping off its map? One way is to sneak in a one-block street that company A knows doesn't exist. If you've doctored your map so that a fake street named Gooby Court falls dead center, you can buy your competitor's map and see if its map features Gooby Court dead center. If it does, well, you'll see *them* in court!

HOME OF THE WHITE SQUIRRELS. It may sound like the motto for a fast-food restaurant that serves up squirrel, but "Home of the White Squirrels" is more likely to be on billboards than menus in three American towns.

That's because Kenton, Tennessee, Olney, Illinois, and Marionville, Missouri, all claim to be the original home of the white squirrel. Kenton says their 200 albino squirrels have been around since the 1860s when gypsies left them behind. Marionville claims their squirrels date from the same time, but that theirs ran away from a traveling circus. Olney isn't saying where their squirrels came from (some Marionville residents say the animals were squirrelnapped from their town), but they know where they are going: everywhere the police go. Olney treasures its critters so much that the police force's badges include an outline of their beloved white squirrel.

HUMAN-SIZED CHECKERBOARD, PETAL, MISSISSIPPI. Venture over to the International Checker Hall of Fame in Petal, Mississippi, when you feel like having a chess player's "Honey, I Shrunk the Kids!" moment.

The hall's basement floor is a sixteen-foot-square

giant checkerboard of green and beige squares. Red or white round pillows serve as the checkers. The Paul Bunyan–sized checkerboard is actually used during world championships to replicate for spectators the moves that the actual competitors are making on their regulation-sized boards.

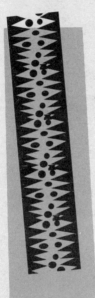

Weird Recess Chatter

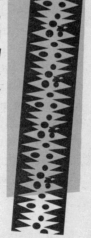

Home of the human string-winding machine. Darwin, Minnesota, lays claim to the worlds largest twine ball. It weighs in at a whopping 21,140 pounds, is twelve feet around, and was the creation of Francis A. Johnson. The ball is housed in a Plexiglas-shielded shed near a city park. A rival claim *could* be made for a twine ball in Cawker City, Kansas. It weighs less but is bigger (forty feet).

Jim Cornfield

INTERNATIONAL BANANA CLUB MUSEUM, ALTADENA, CALIFORNIA. This might be the weirdest museum in the bunch. Just ask Ken "Banana Man" Bannister, the curator of this storefront museum for the past twenty-three years.

Bannister, whose license plate reads THE TB (as in "The Top Banana"), is so wild about bananas that he says he might legally change his name to Bananister some day. Seriously! For now, the fifty-six-year-old former businessman is happy to tend to his 16,500-item collection. Just what's among his bananorabilia? Kid-drawn banana art. Banana-shaped finger puppets. Banana salt and pepper shakers. Banana-shaped squirt guns. A petrified banana. An eighteen-year-old banana. Even a lawn sprinkler shaped like, you guessed it, a banana.

The museum also serves as the worldwide head-quarters for the International Banana Club (banana-loving members range from three months old to 96!). The club holds annual games, as well as contests to see who can snarf the most bananas in the least amount of time. Just in case you're wondering, a forty-three-year-old man is the reigning banana mega-muncher; he gulped eleven six-ounce bananas in *two* minutes. *Bleah!*

But Bannister says you can do more with bananas than eat them or play with them. His tip of the day? Use the inside of a banana peel to shine your dress shoes.

KOBUK VALLEY NATIONAL PARK, ALASKA. What's this? Africa-on-the-Arctic?

They may be located north of the Arctic Circle, but scientists say these thirty square miles of sand bluffs as high as 100 feet are characteristic of sand in the Sahara Desert in Africa. Seems like scientists got some 'splaining to do.

LAKE CHARGOGGAGOGGMANCHAUGGAGOGGCHAUBUNAGUNGAMAUGG, MASSACHUSETTS. Say, what? This forty-five-letter name for a two-square-mile lake near Webster, Massachusetts, is the longest-named place in the United States. The name dates back to the Algonquin Indians. It means, "You fish on your side, we fish on our side; nobody fish in the middle."

The Algonquins knew better than to try and say the

lake's name in one breath. How'd they say it? "Char-gogg-a-gogg...man-chaugg-a-gogg...chaubun-a-gung-a-maugg."

LIBRARY OF NATURAL SOUNDS, ITHACA, NEW YORK. If you want to check out the holdings of this library, you merely have to open your ears—and know what to listen for, such as the sound of ants kicking (yeah, *kicking*!). The surf crashing. Coyotes howling. Whales feeding. These are just a few of the 100,000 recordings on file at Cornell University's Library of Natural Sounds.

To record the sounds of Mother Nature, "recordists" actually go into the wild on a sound hunt. But they aren't armed with guns. They're loaded down with portable tape recorders and funny-looking microphones. (Imagine a two-foot-wide satellite dish, or a black, mannequinlike head with way-sensitive microphones in each ear.) Recordists also have a ton of patience; it often takes as long as 200 hours to get just fifteen *minutes* of usable nature and animal sounds. A lot of tape

"Gee. I can't wait for the CD."

"Yeah. I hear it's a hoot."

is lost to the background sounds of barking dogs, people yapping, or airplanes flying overhead.

But don't think you have to head for Ithaca to hear a whale feeding. Many of the library's recordings can be heard at zoos and museums, on the radio, or at the movies. Just listen up!

Weird Recess Chatter

What shape is the flagpole?

Ohio has the only state flag that isn't square or rectangular. Its flag is shaped like a university pendant with a triangular bite taken out of it.

Q: Why is Ohio shaped funny?

A: Because it's "hi" in the middle and round on both ends!

MAMMOTH CAVE NATIONAL PARK, KENTUCKY.
Everybody knows caves are filled with stalactites and stalagmites and fat-man squeezes. But sick people?

At Kentucky's Mammoth Cave National Park that happened in the 1840s. Several different people owned the cave before it became a national park. One owner, Dr. John Croghan (pronounced "Crawn"), bought the cave in 1839 and opened the Mammoth Cave Sanitarium deep within the cavern. He got the idea to get into the sanitarium business after noticing how invigorated people felt while hiking in the cave. *If healthy people can walk in the cave for miles and miles,* Dr. Croghan thought, *maybe people who have tuberculosis would become healthier if they had a "treatment of cave air."*

For five months Dr. Croghan kept as many as twenty TB patients convalescing down under. He built ten ceilingless (to let in that fresh cave air!) wooden cabins about twelve feet wide and twelve feet long. Two stone huts about seven feet high rounded out the facility. Patients lived in these structures twenty-four hours a day, spread out among cave formations with cool names like Acute Angle and the Bridge of Sighs.

Unfortunately, the cave treatment probably caused more ills than it cured. The temperature fluctuated between a cold thirty degrees and sixty degrees. Fires were used for cooking and for warmth, adding to humidity that was so high that the patients' bedsheets were constantly damp. Not surprisingly, Dr. Croghan's treatment was unsuccessful (in fact, Dr. Croghan himself came down with TB, ultimately dying from the disease).

Here's how the sanitarium looks today. And that's how it appeared back then.

NATIONAL PARKS SERVICE

NATIONAL PARKS SERVICE

"No cable? AND don't even *think* about room service!!!"

If you ever get the chance to tour Mammoth Cave, you can still see two of Dr. Croghan's stone huts when you take the Lantern Tour. Here's a couple of other things worth watching out for. The words O.H.P. ANDERSON, which TB patient Oliver Hazard Perry Anderson wrote into the wall with the smoke of a candle, and the *cough-cough-coughing* of the ghost of a former TB patient named Melissa.

Weird Recess Chatter

"No, don't pack an umbrella." In parts of the Atacama Desert in Chile, it hasn't rained for more than 400 years.

MCDONALD'S, SEDONA, ARIZONA. Don't look for the Golden Arches if you get a McBLT attack while driving through Sedona, Arizona. In Sedona, Mac's arches are teal.

What possessed the hamburgermeisters to ban their trademark rain-slicker-yellow from their signs? Sedona city ordinances. If McDonald's arches hadn't gone teal, they would've had to go green, red, white, or brown. Just remember, the arches may be blue-green, but the catsup's still red.

MOUNT HOREB MUSTARD MUSEUM, MOUNT HOREB, WISCONSIN. Attention all hot dog lovers! If you're sick of squirting the same old yellow stuff on your wiener, head for this mustard mecca. (It's also the home of the (fake) university called "Poupon U!")

The Mount Horeb Mustard Museum displays more than 2,500 different types of mustard. Sure, you'll find American standards like French's. But you'll also find mustard from almost every state and foreign countries as far-flung as Japan, South Africa, and the Czech Republic. More than 150 kinds are available for tasting. Just keep an open mind ("Care for a sample of Prickly Pear Mustard on your hot dog?") and a clear path to the exit. After all, these people put mustard on everything—including ice cream.

Very Punny: "I drove through Mount Horab, but I must-ard missed the museum."

MOUNT RUSHMORE NATIONAL MEMORIAL, SOUTH DAKOTA. What's weird about spending fourteen years and almost a million dollars carving four sixty-foot-tall heads on a 400-foot-high mountain face in the middle of nowhere? Nothing to sculptor Gutzon Borglum, who did just that between 1927 and 1941. But the *really* weird part is what happened in 1931 at the project site.

The presidential lineup was planned to be Jefferson, Washington, Roosevelt, and Lincoln. Borglum had already sculpted Jefferson's hair, forehead, and nose (see 1931 photo, below) when cracks and flaws in the rock became so severe that Jefferson's likeness had to be moved. So, *ka-boom!* The sculptor blasted off Jefferson's face and resculpted it on Washington's left. Today the lineup is Washington, Jefferson, Roosevelt, and Lincoln.

NATIONAL PARKS SERVICE

NATIONAL PARKS SERVICE

Here's how Mt. Rushmore appears today. But that's not how it was planned. In fact, the story behind it is a real . . .

blast.

OREGON VORTEX, GOLD HILL, OREGON. This "atmospheric whirlpool" in southeastern Oregon will make you question what you see. Invisible magnetic lines create a 165-foot circle of force known as the Vortex. Half of the magnetic field lies above the ground, half below. Eye-boggling stuff happens in the middle of that circle.

Face south, for instance, and you *look* a couple of inches shorter than when you face north. In some places, a ball seems to defy gravity and roll uphill. Even trees in the Vortex tilt toward magnetic north! Some people believe the electric and magnetic fields in the area act as a sort of electron lens, focusing streams of electrons the way a glass lens focuses light rays. So looking at some places inside the Vortex is like looking through a weird magnifying lens.

Long ago, Indians sensed that the land near what's now known as the Vortex was, well, exceptionally spooked. That's why they called the area the Forbidden Ground. When forced to camp overnight there, Indians noticed that their horses stayed skittish all night long!

OTTO ORKIN INSECT ZOO, WASHINGTON, D.C. Other zoos may have bigger animals, but creatures here have the most legs.

The Otto Orkin Insect Zoo exhibits more than sixty species of live insects at the zoo—and several hundred dead ones. The lineup includes millipedes, centipedes, cockroaches, ants, walking sticks, termites, crickets, spiders, tarantulas, mosquitoes, and silverfish.

Like most zoos, though, feeding time and petting time are big draws. Three times a day, you can watch zookeepers feed tarantulas their one-cricket meals. Petting time is enough to make you squirm. Unless, of course, you're used to having a two-inch-long Madagascar Hissing cockroach inch up your arm.

For a real Indiana Jones moment, crawl through an African termite mound that tops out at fourteen feet. The piped-in sound of termites munching and crunching will absolutely make your skin crawl!

Weird Recess Chatter

Bug weight. What weighs as much as 1,600,000 fruit flies? You might! Step on a scale at the Insectarium in Philadelphia, Pennsylvania, and you'll find out your weight in ladybugs, fruit flys, or lightning bugs!

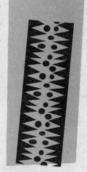

PLANET HOLLYWOOD. These Hollywood-themed restaurants owned by actors Arnold Schwarzenegger, Sly Stallone, and Bruce Willis would have a hard time selling T-shirts with the eatery's *real* name. The official name, as it would appear on the front (and back) of a T-shirt? Try, "The Only Ordinary People Trying to Impress the Big Guys with Extraordinary Ideas, Sales, Management, Creative Thinking and Problem Solving Consultancy Company Ltd."

ROUTE 46, NEAR FARGO, NORTH DAKOTA.
"Look, Ma, no hands!"

That's what you'd say if you were old enough to drive and smart enough to find this no-winder of a highway. This is the longest *straight* stretch of road in the country. Road warriors can drive 110 miles without having to adjust their steering.

SCOTLAND YARD OF ANIMAL CRIME, ASHLAND, OREGON. Okay, so maybe that's just the *nickname* for the world's most bizarre crime lab. Its official name is the National Fish and Wildlife Forensics Laboratory. Yeah, you guessed it, it only solves crimes against animals.

Here's the facts, ma'am. The lab's job is to figure out how, when, and where animal corpses from around the world were killed. The victims don't arrive by ambulance; they come via UPS from all fifty states and 130 foreign countries. Using such evidence as a strand of hair, a single tooth, or a piece of meat, the thirty-one-member crew identifies their animal victims. (They can identify a rare bird from just a single feather!) Other clues come from analyzing the DNA of an animal's hide or blood.

The lab has solved some pretty weird crimes. They figured out who'd slaughtered 400 headless walruses that washed up in Alaska (Eskimo poachers who were illegally selling the walruses' tusks). In another case, an agent dressed in a gorilla costume got to the bottom of a monkey-stealing scam (a Mexican zoo was involved!).

The state-of-the-art crime lab has the usual crime-fighting equipment, along with a few oddities most human crime labs don't have. Like, a floor-to-ceiling freezer to store dead eagles, and a warehouse to stash some 300,000 items—stuff like tigerskin rugs and snakeskin shoes and elephant-foot footstools—made from illegally killed animals. For the animals delivered here, the lab delivers final justice.

STRAIT OF MALACCA, INDIAN OCEAN. You thought all that "Shiver me timbers" stuff was history? Not so fast, matey. The Strait of Malacca, off Singapore in the Indian Ocean, is *currently* the most pirate-infested stretch of water in the world.

Modern-day Blackbeards use speedboats to zip aboard slower-moving freight ships. Once aboard, they put a gun to the captain's head, make him open the ship's safe (it often has as much as $50,000 in it to cover months of expenses), and force the unarmed crew to row to shore. Then the pirates steal whatever the ship is transporting: VCRs, motorcycles, sugar, coffee, steel. They resell the cargo for tens of thousands of dollars.

Punishable by death? Hope they don't have to walk the plank!

The Strait of Malacca is so pirate-prone because about 240 ships a day must pass through it and there are lots of little uninhabited islands nearby where pirates can hide. Too bad pirates don't do their monkey business in international waters. If they did, their crimes would be punishable by death.

Weird Recess Chatter

"Does **it stop** at **every dirt** level?" The "Stratavator" at the Carnegie Museum of Natural History in Pittsburgh takes museum-goers on a wild ride down under. It takes passengers down through 16,000 feet of tunnel underneath the city.

TORNADO ALLEY. Tornadoes have put some states on the map. Texas, Oklahoma, Kansas, Missouri, and Iowa—together nicknamed Tornado Alley—are the most tornado-struck states in America. In fact, about a third of the tornadoes that annually strike the United States touch down in Texas, Oklahoma, and Kansas!

The Great Plains are primed for tornados because warm, wet air from the Gulf of Mexico hits cooler, drier air from the Rocky Mountains. The result? Scenes straight out of *The Wizard of Oz.*

Skies darken as black as a burning building's smoke. Hail the size of Ping-Pong balls falls. Winds blow as fast as 300 miles per hour. Houses and cars get sucked into tornado funnels as wide as 600 feet. Family heirlooms can be blown forty miles from home. Trucks somersault down expressways.

In May, the height of tornado season, stormaholics flock to Tornado Alley. Amateur and professional tornado chasers with cool nicknames like "Thunderhead" think nothing of driving more than 10,000 miles in two weeks, crisscrossing the area in search of twisters.

Weird Recess Chatter

Twister

trivia. Most tornados in the northern hemisphere rotate counterclockwise. Only one in a thousand spins clockwise.

UNDERGROUND VAULTS AND STORAGE, HUTCHIN-SON, KANSAS. Need a top-secret stash to protect something you treasure? Send it to the salt mines.

The thirty-five-acre Undergound Vaults and Storage in Hutchinson, Kansas, rents out space 650 feet belowground in an active salt mine. Valuables are kept in the mine's perfect climate: sixty-eight degrees and fifty percent humidity. One movie mogul stores his original reels of *The Wizard of Oz, Gone With the Wind,* and *Mutiny on the Bounty.* Somebody else has 17,000 Bibles shelved here! Another client keeps his

Stradivarius violin. Needless to say, security below-ground is way *above* average.

U.S. NATIONAL TICK COLLECTION, STATESBORO, GEORGIA. Head for Georgia Southern University if ticks make you tick. No, the little eight-leggers aren't in class there; they're in vials!

The collection includes 760 specimens (yeah, they're dead) of the 850 species known worldwide that can carry such diseases as Rocky Mountain Spotted Fever. Each specimen notes where the tick was found, when it was found, what it likes to live on, who found it, its species, and an ID number. So far, more than a million ticks are floating around (literally, in alcohol) at GSU.

The United States isn't the only country that keeps tabs on ticks. Britain, Russia, and South Africa have tick collections, too.

*Very Punny:
Ever wonder what makes
this museum tick?*

WINCHESTER MYSTERY HOUSE, SAN JOSE, CALIFORNIA. The spirits made her do it! That's how rifle heiress Sara Winchester explained a thirty-eight-year-long home remodeling project that turned her eight-room farmhouse into this 160-room spookorama.

Here's how the whole thing happened. In 1884, Winchester went to a psychic who told her that the spirits of all the people who had been killed with Winchester rifles were hopping mad at her. So mad, in fact, that they had placed a curse on her. (Winchester had reason to believe the curse part: both her baby daughter and her husband had died.) The ghosts were going to haunt her forever unless she moved west, bought a house, and added to it as the ghosts directed. So, Winchester moved to California. She bought a $13,000 farmhouse, and she started the renovations that would end up taking thirty-eight years and costing $5.5 million!

Thanks to her ghostly architects, Winchester ended up with a house fit for a phantom. Staircases dead-end at ceilings. Doors open to solid walls. Many rooms have thirteen windows, each with thirteen panes of glass. Chandeliers have thirteen lights. If ghosts are anywhere, chances are they're floating around this spook-friendly city! Check it out for yourself; 110 rooms are open to the public.

YORK, ENGLAND. If you're into ghostly weirdness, head for the place that ghostbusters call the most haunted city in Europe: York, in the north of England.

What makes York so spooky? Fourteenth-century stone walls, complete with a walkway, surround the city and give townspeople a bird's-eye view of a number of haunted buildings. Townspeople have heard the sound of a trumpet fanfare, then looked up to see marching soldiers decked out in Roman uniforms that date from the first century. Oh, yeah, the soldiers are *invisible from the knees down!* Ghostbusters say this makes perfect sense because the soldiers are marching on York's original road, buried beneath the current one.

But wait, there's more! A 300-year-old ghost supposedly haunts the Treasurer's house. The Yorkminster cathedral is haunted by a man named Dean Gale, who still likes to sit in his family pew. The Theatre Royal has a ghost known as the Grey Lady. And the city library is spooked by an old man. Even the ghost of Charles I keeps reappearing in a stairway! Steer clear of York if you don't want ghosts to make your day.

"Hmm . . . Now, that's really weird!"

the Weird list

A lot of states have weird names. Have you ever wondered, for example, who dreamed up the word "Wisconsin?" Take a look at the origins of some of the weirdest-named states.

State	Indian word	Tribe	What it means
Connecticut	"quinnetikq-ut"	Mohican	"at the big tidal river"
Idaho	"Ee-dah-how"	Shoshone	"Look, the sun is coming down the mountain!"
Iowa	"ouaouiatonon"	Dakota	"sleepy ones."
Kentucky	"ken-tah-teh"	Cherokee	"land of tomorrow"
Massachusetts	"massa-wachuset"	Algonquin	"great hill"
Michigan	"michi-gama"	Ojibway	"great water"
Minnesota	"minn-sota"	Dakota	"sky-tinted water"
Mississippi	"mescha-cebe"	Algonquin	"great water"
Missouri	"missouri"	Dakota	"people with the long canoes"
Wisconsin	"wees-kon-san"	Ojibway	"gathering of waters"

People

BABE RUTH. He might have been the greatest baseball player ever, but Babe Ruth sure had a weird way of keeping cool.

The New York Yankee star wet down cabbage leaves and stuck them under his ballcap to keep the hot sun from heating his head!

"Hey, Babe! How 'bout some corned beef with that cabbage!"

AIRSICKNESS-BAG COLLECTOR BEN GUTTERY. Toss your cookies in Ben Guttery's Fort Worth, Texas, house and you won't have to worry about ruining the rug. He collects airline barf bags. *Tons* of them.

Guttery has a 1,060-bag collection from more that 400 different airlines! He's got airsickness bags from the usual suspects—American Airlines, Delta, United—and even more from such obscure airlines as China Southwest and Azerbaijani Airlines. Most of the bags are paper, but a few are plastic. The German airline Saxonia, for example, provides a plastic bag with its own lid! (He especially values bags that are unusual or historical.) Guttery spends a couple of hours a week writing airlines and other collectors worldwide in search of bags to round out his collection.

A four-inch-wide, six-inch-tall paper cup that American Airlines used in the twenties is the barforabilia he's most after now. Something tells us Guttery won't throw up his hands till the cup is in his collection.

CASTLE BUILDER JIM BISHOP. A lot of people want their home to be their castle. Businessman Jim Bishop just wants a castle to call home. That's why he's spent every spare minute for the last twenty-seven years building Bishop Castle off Highway 165 near Rye, Colorado.

So far the castle is 160-feet tall with three towers, onion-shaped domes, and a smoke-breathing dragon. But Bishop has plans. Big plans! He wants to add a mountain tunnel and a balcony huge enough to fit a symphony. For now Bishop, his wife, and four kids live in a regular house in nearby Pueblo, Colorado. No word yet on whether an authentic English maze will find a place in this a-mazing palace!

CROSS-DRESSING CIVIL WAR SOLDIERS. Uncle Sam has always said he wanted a few good men. What he was unaware of was that he was getting quite a few good *women,* too. In the 1860s, women masqueraded as men so that they could fight in the Civil War.

the Weird INTERVIEW: Ben Guttery

Q: Are you the only guy in the whole wide world who collects airline barf bags?

A: "No, there are about twenty-five other barf bag collectors in the world. We all keep in touch. There's a fellow in his sixties in the Netherlands who has about twice as many as I do. He's the one to beat!"

Q: Which bag in your collection was toughest to get?

A: "The Burma Airways bag. Burma is such an extremely exotic place that I've only met one person who's ever flown on Burma Airways."

Q: What are the biggest and smallest bags in your collection?

A: "The old National Airlines barf bag is about the size of a grocery store bag; it's plastic. They folded it four times. The smallest bag is from an airline in the family of Air Indonesia called Garuda. The bag is only about four inches by six inches."

Q: What's the funniest bag you've got?

A: "There is a funny one that came out in the early eighties from Sun Airlines in California. It says, IF YOU CAN USE THIS BAG QUIETLY, YOU CAN BECOME A MEMBER OF THE QUYAT ERP BARFING SOCIETY."

Q: When you're at a party and you tell people that you collect barf bags, what do they say?

A: "They always say, 'New or used?' I must have heard that joke a million times. Actually, the only used one I have is from an airline in Libya. It has a piece of chewed gum at the bottom of it."

More than 125 cases of cross-dressing female soldiers have been documented so far. An Illinois regiment included a soldier named Albert D. J. Cashier. Or so they thought. Al's *real* name was Jennie. As in Jennie Hodges. In Michigan, Sarah Emma Edmonds became Franklin Thompson to serve with the infantry. In New York, Sarah Rosetta Wakeman became Private Lyons Wakeman and was stationed in Alexandria, Virginia. And on and on. The actual number of women who disguised themselves as men and enlisted could be more than 400.

Why were women so eager to be on the front lines of battle? Some wanted to have an adventurous life. Others didn't want to be separated from their enlisted boyfriends or husbands. Still others wanted the payoff at the end of their service: a military pension.

So just how could the typical military man not realize that the guy next to him was really a gal? For starters, so many boys were in the military that a small-boned "man" without a beard was assumed to be a boy in his early teens. Plus, recruits rarely undressed totally—not even during physicals!—and baths and showers were few and far between. If a female soldier bound down her breasts and wore her hair short, she pretty much could pass for a he.

Until, that is, she got wounded and wound up at an army hospital. Off came the boots! Off came the uniform! Whoa! Once a soldier was discovered to be female, she was discharged. Uncle Sam was dead serious about a soldier's gender.

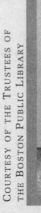

DR. BUKK. Most people get false teeth to *improve* their smile. Then there's the kind of fake teeth Nancy "Dr. Bukk" Albert makes. Her teeth turn a person's normal-looking chops into every dentist's nightmare.

Dr. Bukk (as in "buckteeth," get it?) got the idea in 1982 when she saw how much fun a dentist friend had when he popped in dentures that purposely turned his pearly whites into tobacco-stained yellows. Albert wanted a set, too, but the dentist she went to wanted about $400 to make them. That's when the freelance artist decided to create her own.

Dr. Bukk's teeth are made from plastic and fashioned into one of fourteen styles. The gums are pink, but look infected! The teeth are misshapened and stained. Want tobacco-stained teeth? Smokers is the model for you; it's got tar-stained teeth with three corroded spaces big enough to stick a cig through. Wanna look like you needed a retainer, oh, about five years ago? Get the buckiest model, the Flagship Bukk, or the new Cowcatcher, which has nine yellow-stained, horsey teeth that splay out at a 45-degree angle.

Since 1989, Albert has sold more than 20,000 sets of teeth to average Joes as well as celebrities such as singer Jimmy Buffet, actor John Goodman, and military hero Captain Scott O'Grady. Guess if you can afford to get your teeth fixed, it just might be more fun if you didn't.

DR. PUMPKINSTEIN. Now this is a pumpkin grower Paul Bunyan would love.

For ten years, Rick "Dr. Pumpkinstein" Dickow of

NANCY ALBERT

← Before

After?

!!!→

NANCY ALBERT

Menlo Park, California, has grown pumpkins that have literally outgrown him. Just how much does a typical Dr. Pumpkinstein pumpkin weigh? Try a squashing 595 pounds!

When Dr. Pumpkinstein competes in the World Pumpkin Confederation's annual weigh-in, he always takes along a stethoscope to keep the contestants honest. (Less-than-honest pumpkin growers can pump a pumpkin full of water to make it heavier and tip the scales.) Dr. Pumpkinstein rocks a pumpkin, holds his stethoscope against it, and listens for sounds of sloshing. No sloshing, no problem. Guess even pumpkin growers need to be good gumshoes.

the Weird INTERVIEW: Dr. Bukk

Q: You make plastic teeth for people who want to turn their good teeth into gnarly ones. Why would anyone want to wear bad teeth?

A: "Some people think it's to make fun of people with bad teeth, but it's really just for fun. It's a different way to experience ordinary activities like making a bank deposit or going shopping. It's fun to watch the reaction of the people waiting on you."

Q: What's a typical reaction?

A: "People will cover their own mouth with their hand or be nice to you face-to-face, then whoop and laugh when they think you're beyond earshot."

Q: What are some of your weirdest models?

A: "The Gnarly, which makes your teeth look like you've been riding a motorcycle too closely behind a gravel truck. The Zipper, which has three or four extra teeth jammed together. The Chikklets, which has two great big front teeth with a big gap between them and small gaps between the smaller teeth."

Q: What kind of people are your best clients?

A: "Fighter pilots! A lot of times thirty or forty fighter pilots from the same base will place an order. We call that 'doin' a base.' We've also done teeth for loads and loads of attorneys and stockbrokers."

Q: How can you fit people when they live all over the world?

A: "People bite down on a piece of Styrofoam from coffee cups, then they mail in their bite marks. They can even fax them to me. We send them the teeth, with instructions on how to mold them with the steam from a tea kettle. Once the teeth are customized, they'll only fit you. Bukk teeth fit so well they'd fool your own mother!"

"DUGOUT" DICK ZIMMERMAN. Call him modern-day caveman.

Prospector Dick Zimmerman does something strange to a mine when he's done digging for minerals in it: he turns the cave into a hermit's version of a Motel 6. His Dugout Ranch near Salmon, Idaho, has ten "rooms," each complete with a recycled door and a window that used to be a windshield on a car. Other creature comforts in the $2-a-night room include a school-bus seat that serves as a makeshift couch. Sounds comfy, but we'd better pass!

EKINS. No, this isn't the secret name for some weird group of people who are super-scared of mice. It's what super-loyal workers at megashoe manufacturer Nike call themselves (Nike spelled backward is Ekin, get it?).

Weirder still is what a lot of Ekins have done in each other's company to show their company spirit. They get Nike's trademark "swoosh" tattooed on their calf or on their upper thigh. Wonder what's next? A giraffe-tattooed "Usrsyots" group for Toys 'R' Us employees? Stay tuned.

Weird Recess Chatter

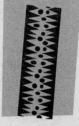

"Get **up**, Dad! You're **sitting** on Jessie, **again!**" One in six kids has had an imaginary friend at some point during his or her childhood.

GRASS ARTIST GENE POOL. Some artists work with paint. Others prefer clay. Artist Gene Pool's medium is Manhattan Perennial Rye #2. As in grass. (Yeah, the kind you mow!)

Pool puts adhesive down on his soon-to-be-mowable creations, covers the glue with grass seed, waters, wraps it in plastic, and waits two weeks while the green stuff grows. The insta-sod stays picture perfect for about two weeks. So far the Brooklyn grassoholic has seeded a briefcase, suits, shoes, hats, and two Buick Le Sabres! His cars may never need washing, but mowing is another matter.

Very Punny:
A grass-covered car?
Wonder if he ever got
stopped for a mowing
violation?

GROSSOLOGIST SYLVIA BRANZEI. Science educator Sylvia Branzei loves it when people talk gross to her. After all, she wrote the book on the subject, *Grossology: The Science of Really Gross Things.*

Branzei's brush with grossness goes back to when she was a kid. She taught herself how to burp on command. She knew by heart all the songs with the words "diarrhea" in them. She learned how to say "poop" in several foreign languages. So what's a kid grossologist to become when she grows up? Try a microbiology major and a science teacher. Now she's

the Weird INTERVIEW: Gene Pool

Q: Is it hard to grow grass on, say, a suit?

A: "No. I take organic glue and put it on the suit. Then I stick on the seeds and cover it with a plastic bag. I water the seeds three times a day till they sprout, which usually takes about forty-eight hours. Then it takes two more weeks until the grass is full grown. The grass lasts for another couple of weeks."

Q: What's the biggest project that you've ever grown?

A: "I grew grass on twenty-five robes for the Twenty-fifth Anniversary of Earth Day."

Q: Cool! Does it matter what kind of grass you use?

A: "First I tried Kentucky Bluegrass, but it took thirty days to germinate, so it didn't work. Then I switched to Manhattan Perennial Rye #2, which germinates in forty-eight hours. I've been using that ever since. There's another kind of grass called Bright Star that is a greener green. I used it to grow the Earth Day robes."

Q: What's the weirdest thing that's ever happened to you when you've been in your grass-covered car?

A: "I used to grow grass on a 1966 Buick Le Sabre. This is when I lived in Kansas City. The police pulled me over one time because they said the grass was too long on the back of the car. They made me get out of my car and clip the grass around the taillights!"

Q: Do you think you'll ever get tired of making grass grow on stuff?

A: "Well, I'm branching out to other things. I'm in the middle of making a suit out of winebottle corks. I'm gonna float in it someplace fun. Or maybe in a swimming pool!"

researching all things gross for her upcoming books *Animal Grossology* (ticks, lice, etc.) and *Grossology II,* which will cover such gnarly subjects as constipation, toe jam, and rashes.

So what's the grossest part about being a grossologist? "Everybody tells me their grossest stories and sends me gross mail," Branzei says. "Kids will say, 'Last year I was in the backseat of the car with my sister and she did a projectile barf and it splattered all over the front window!' My own sister had her earwax suctioned. What'd she do with the earwax? She sent it to me." Now *that's* gross!

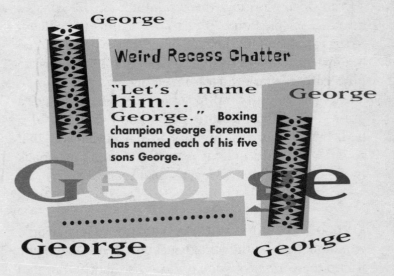

George

Weird Recess Chatter

"Let's name **him...** George." Boxing champion George Foreman has named each of his five sons George.

George

George

George

George

HOAXMEISTER JOEY SKAGGS. Call Joey Skaggs the Great Pretender. Skaggs has spent the last thirty years pretending to be people he's not. Why? To dupe the media—and teach the public that you can't always believe what you read in the newspaper or see on TV.

As Jo-Jo, King of the Gypsies, Skaggs protested that the gypsy moth's name was insulting to real Gypsies. As Kea So Joo ("Dog Meat Soup" in Korean), he mailed 1,500 letters that proposed buying stray dogs and then turning them into canned food (to make his scam more believable, he even set up a fake corporate phone line and recorded a message on it in both Korean and English, with barking dogs in the background). One New York City TV station used the story to open its ten o'clock news show!

Even *Good Morning America* fell for one of Skaggs's hoaxes. As Joe Bones, the leader of the Fat Squad, Skaggs appeared on the morning TV show and offered to move in with overweight people (for $300 a day) to physically restrain them from eating.

After successfully pulling off a hoax, Skaggs issues a press release that lets the media know that it's been had. If you ever read a story in the newspaper that sounds too weird to be true, you just might be smack in the middle of Joey Skaggs's next scam.

KING OF RECORDS ASHRITA FURMAN. Most people would feel cool if they broke just one record and made it into the *Guinness Book of Records.* Ashrita Furman has done that so often it's routine. He's the recordholder for having the most records.

Say, what? Furman, at forty-one years old, has a dozen records under his belt. He's played 307 hopscotch games—one after the other—in twenty-four hours. He's balanced a milk bottle on his noggin for—*splash!*—seventy miles. He's lugged a nine-pound brick in one hand for sixty-four miles. He's also pogo-sticked for three hours and forty minutes in the piranha-infested Amazon River. And he's set a clapping record. Guinness on!

LE PETOMANE. If French entertainer Joseph Pujol were around today instead of in the late-1800s, when he actually lived, he would probably be known simply as Fartman. As it was, his nickname in French was Le Petomane. Translation? The Fartomaniac.

Able to create different sounds of varying length, Pujol took his act to the stage and to the palaces of European royalty. Not that the French had a total monopoly on such a weird talent. Japan had a fartman of its own, too. In 1980 the unnamed performer went on TV and passed gas more than 3,000 times in a row!

MEGAGROUP PHOTOGRAPHER ARTHUR MOLE. There are group pictures and there are *group* pictures. During and right after World War I, commercial photographer Arthur Mole took the ultimate group pics; his portraits called for as many as 30,000 soldiers to pose at a time!

Mole called his pictures "living photographs." Here was his drill: he went to an empty field, used miles of lace to rope off outlines of patriotic images such as the Liberty Bell and the Statue of Liberty, and crammed thousands and thousands of soldiers into the half-mile-tall shapes. Then he climbed an 80-foot tower and looked through his camera lens at his masterpiece. Soldiers in dark uniforms and dark hats "became" navy stripes! Soldiers in white shirts "turned into" white stripes!

So just how many military men did it take Mole to create a masterpiece? Try 30,000 troops to create a police-badge-shaped United States shield. Some 21,000 men and women stood shoulder to shoulder to depict a 700-foot-tall portrait of then-President Woodrow Wilson's head and shoulders. It took 25,000 men to become a dead ringer for the Liberty Bell and 18,000 troops to form the human Statue of Liberty. Because these Kodak moments took hours and hours to produce, Mole couldn't use just anyone as models. Military men were the only people disciplined enough to stand like statues for hours on end. *"TEN-tion!!"*

MENTAWAI. If Dracula found himself flashing a grin among the Mentawai, a tribe of native people who live on the island of Siberut off the west coast of Sumatra in Indonesia, nobody would scream. Instead, he'd most likely get a pointy-toothed smile flashed right back at him.

When young Mentawai men and women reach their twenties, they are allowed to have their upper front four teeth filed down into points. The procedure is done with a knife, so it takes a few hours and is pretty painful. Pointed teeth supposedly make bone crunching easier and, believe the Mentawai, please the soul.

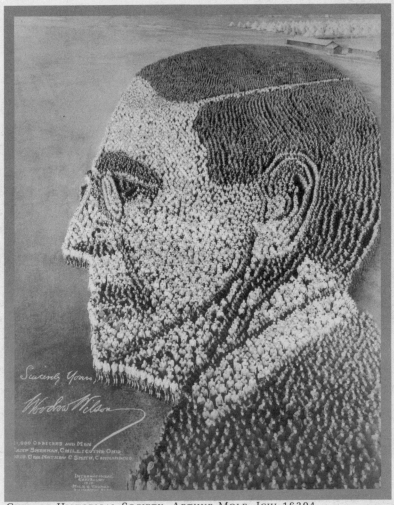

CHICAGO HISTORICAL SOCIETY, ARTHUR MOLE, ICHI-16304

"Okay.
Everyone smile and
say "CHEESE!"
CHEESE!!!!

NAVAJO CODE TALKERS. Who would you turn to to come up with a secret code that a military enemy would find impossible to crack? During World War II, the Marine Corps sought help from a weird source: Navajo Indians.

Navajo was the ideal language for soldiers to send messages in because it had no written equivalent. Twenty-nine Navajo Marines invented a top-secret code that would grow to a vocabulary of 508 words. They taught it to incoming Navajo Marines, whose Native American culture stresses memorization. Eventually, some 400 Navajo Code Talkers, as they came to be known, served in the war against Japan, taking part in every Marine assault in the Pacific from 1942 to 1945.

When the Navajo Marines went to the Pacific, their code books stayed in the States. They had to memorize everything! Top secret information was transmitted Navajo to Navajo, then translated for English-speaking commanding officers. Here's how it worked: A code talker would receive a message. But it didn't make sense, just random-seeming Navajo words strung together. When each word was translated into its English equivalent, the first letter of *those* words were used to spell out an English word. For instance, the Navajo words *"be-la-sana"* (apple) and *"tse nill"* (axe) could both stand for the letter "a".

Whew...sounds confusing. Of course, not all words had to be spelled out this way: Navajos called cruisers *"Lo-tso-yazzle,"* or "small whales." They called an amphibious piece of equipment *"chal,"* or a frog. A transport plane was *"Dineh-nay-ye-hi,"* or a "man carrier." The United States became *"Nihi-mah,"* or "our mother." Who would have thought an ancient language would become the source of a code that our military enemies could never crack?

Weird Recess Chatter

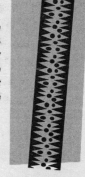

"Honey, can I get in line one more time!" Who's the Roller Coaster King at Paramount's Kings Island in Kings Island, Ohio? Try a store manager who's ridden the Racer more than 8,000 times (he didn't even toss his cookies until he rode the Racer for the 7,211th time!).

PETER THE GREAT OF RUSSIA. What would you do if the President of the United States came up to you while you were riding your bike, complimented you on how fast you could pedal it, then demanded to pull one of your teeth for his collection? If you lived in Russia in the late 1600s, you would stand still while your tooth was yanked from your mouth!

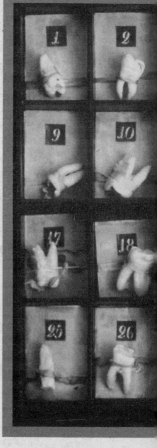

That's just how Peter the Great of Russia (1672–1725) acquired one of the weirdest collections of his *kunstkammer,* or chamber of curiosities, much of which can still be viewed at the Leningrad Museum in Russia.

Emperor Peter didn't like to save his own molars; he liked to personally pull teeth out of other people's mouths. A messenger who was an extremely fast walker lost a tooth to Peter. So did a singer, a tablecloth-maker, a bishop, and the emperor's own nurse! And lots more! Peter stored his toothly treasures in a beautiful wooden case. Each tooth was secured to its own little compartment with a gray silk ribbon looped around it. An exquisitely written number was penned above each tooth; each number matched the number on a list that detailed the profession of the person who lost the tooth. Thank goodness he didn't have a fondness for fingers. *Ouch!*

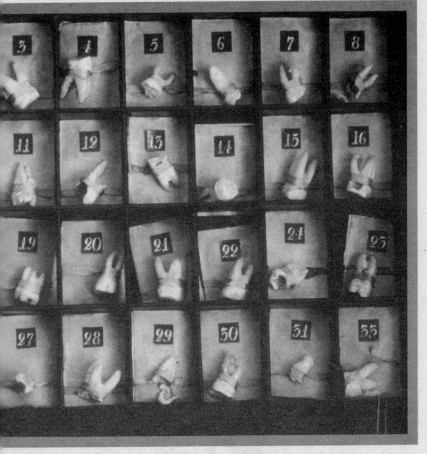

Very Punny: He pulled the tooth.
The whole tooth.
And Nothing but the tooth.

SELF-OPERATING SURGEON EVAN O'NEILL KANE, M.D. Most people can cover their own cuts with Band-Aids or remove a splinter from a finger with tweezers. But amputate their own finger? Take out their own appendix? No way!

Dr. Evan O'Neill Kane of Kane, Pennsylvania, did just that and more. In 1919 he cut off an injured finger on his own hand. Two years later, he took out his own appendix, a small saclike appendage that's attached to the large intestine. When Dr. Kane was seventy, he repaired his own hernia, a part of the intestine that can rupture through abdominal muscles. Thank goodness he never needed open-heart surgery!

"Dr. Kane . . . you can see yourself now!"

THE HUMAN LIGHTNING CONDUCTOR. Ex–park ranger Roy C. Sullivan didn't like to be told that lightning never hit the same place twice. Sullivan was struck by lightning seven times over thirty-five years, a distinction that earned him the title of "The Human Lightning Conductor" of Virginia.

Each time ranger Sullivan walked away from the scene of a strike, he walked off with a little less of himself. He lost his big toenail when he was struck by lightning in 1942. He lost his eyebrows when he was hit in 1969. Sullivan's left shoulder was seared in 1970. Two years later, his hair was set afire. He was struck on the head in 1973. His hair *and* legs were seared in 1976. Finally, Sullivan sustained chest and stomach burns in 1977 after being struck while fishing.

Considering that the odds of being injured by lightning during your lifetime are one in 9,100, Sullivan was hit about seven times more than he should have been, before his death in 1983. Too bad insurance companies don't sell lightning insurance for people.

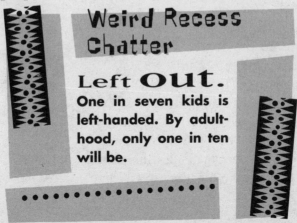

Weird Recess Chatter

Left **out.**

One in seven kids is left-handed. By adulthood, only one in ten will be.

THE DEAN OF WEIRD NEWS. MAN KILLED IN ARGUMENT OVER HOT DOG! That's the kind of headline that gets the attention of Chuck Shepherd, an ex–business-law professor at George Washington University in Washington, D.C. Shepherd has an interesting hobby: he collects weird news.

For almost twenty years, Shepherd has clipped, color-coded, and filed thousands and thousands of bizarre and odd news items. Such as the story about the Japanese company that offered a "Dial-a-Flattery" service to people who didn't get complimented enough. Or the clip that featured the Swedish maintenance man who assaulted 632 people by speeding up a moving sidewalk to fifty miles an hour!

He turns his tidbits into material for his newsletters, syndicated "News of the Weird" column, and *News of the Weird* books. Some news he lets rattle around in his head, like the fact that cats get left more money from their deceased owners than dogs. Birds—in case you're a junior weird-news collector—come in third.

THE WOMAN WITH TEN BRAINS. Her real name was Thea Alba, but she became famous in the 1920s as the Woman with Ten Brains.

Of course, this German woman really had only *one* brain. The reason why people thought Alba had multiple brains was due to her stage act. She would entertain people by attaching a long pointer (picture a paintbrush with chalk at the end instead of bristles) to each of her fingers and writing ten different letters at the same time!

Another part of her act was more dramatic to watch. She would recline in a special chair on stage, her back to the audience, with three blackboards within arm's reach that faced the audience. On cue, her limbs *simultaneously* went into spelling mode. Her left hand wrote Tokyo. Her left foot, decked out in an elf-shoe–like device with chalk attached at the point, wrote Rome. Her right foot, London. Her right hand spelled out Paris. She could even write different sentences in French, German, and English at the same time. With talent like that, who needs an extra nine brains?

WEIRD STUFF BUYER JOHN TURNER. Do you know someone who's got something really, really weird that they're ready to get rid of? Like, say, a 167-piece bedpan collection? Or a six-ton ball of string?

People who really had those items knew who to call: John Turner, the curator of artifacts for Ripley's Believe It or Not! He flies more than 100,000 miles a year in search of weird stuff (yeah, he actually bought a 167-piece bedpan collection and a monster-sized ball of string!) for Ripley's twenty-one museums worldwide. Wonder where he found the portrait of Mona Lisa made of toast?

Meet Ripper, the Friendly Shark!

CREATED BY TOM KENNEDY, PHOTOGRAPH BY HARROD BLANK

Lifestyles

Now that's what we call "losing your head."

ANCIENT HEAD PROTECTION. Before metal helmets were invented for warfare, some soldiers protected their noggins from the inside out. Say what?

Indians who lived in what is now the Caribbean lashed slabs of wood to the foreheads of male babies in the tribe. No, it wasn't an early form of child abuse. The slabs thickened the skull bones so that the future warriors would survive an arrow to the head.

ART CARS. Most people personalize their vehicles in a low-key sort of way. They hang something from the rearview mirror or put a PROUD PARENT OF A HIGH SCHOOL DROPOUT! sticker on their bumper. But every once in a while you run across a car whose owner has turned it into a moving masterpiece.

HARROD BLANK,
WILD WHEELS

Called art cars, these one-of-a-kind vehicles (there are about 300 in the country) are decorated into weird works of art. Take the *Hippomobile*. Six hundred pounds of copper sheeting turned this former 1971 Ford Mustang convertible into a dead ringer for a giant hippopotamus (a built-in PA system plays hippo grunts to complete that "on safari" feeling).

Weird Recess Chatter

Floating
monsters? Monster trucks—those souped-up passenger trucks atop wheels as tall as ten feet—float in water! All the air in those ten-foot-tall tires make monster trucks the perfect automotive life preserver.

BARBERS. Here's a snippet of history that just might make you queasy. If you lived in England in the seventh century and you had bad hair, bad teeth, or a bad heart, you would have sought help from the same person: the barber!

Barbers kind of "fell into" doing medical procedures. Here's the long and short of it: the church required men to get the crowns of their heads shaved when they joined a monastery. Naturally, the monks-to-be called on the monastery's barber-in-residence to do the deed. Other church rituals called for a barber to cut open a person's veins to remove "bad blood."

In 1372 the king's barber talked Charles the Wise into letting barbers treat wounds and sores. Barbers still shaved heads, but they started amputating limbs and pulling teeth, too. Even physicians hired barber-surgeons (called "Surgeons of the Short Robe") to do routine surgeries on their patients. Finally, in 1745, barbers and surgeons were legally separated in England; only physicians could practice medicine and operate on people.

Pass any barbershop today and you'll see a reminder of the profession's bloody past. See that red- and white-striped barber pole? After medieval barbers finished their operations, they wrapped their blood-stained white bandages around the pole nearest their office. Today's candy cane–striped barber poles date back to that practice!

"Today's special includes a haircut and an appendectomy!"

Weird Recess Chatter

Paper clip clip.

Twenty *billion* paper clips are produced each year; about a third of them get lost.

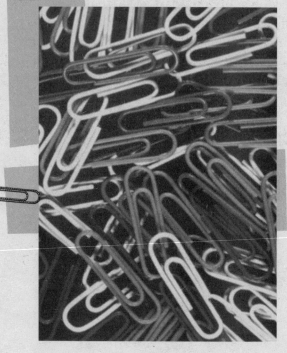

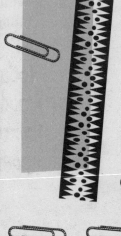

BARREL JUMPING. If Evel Knievel was into winter sports, *this* would be the one he'd do!

Barrel jumpers speed-skate around an ice rink a couple of times till they're going about thirty miles per hour. Then they whip their arms up like they're sleepwalk-ing, and *ju-u-u-ump!* The goal is to leap over as many fiber-glass barrels laid side-by-side on the ice as they can.

OK. But will it be an Olympic sport?

(The world record is a mind-boggling eighteen-barrel jump!) But don't expect to see a Nancy Kerrigan–picture-perfect landing. Barrel jumpers usually land on their butts, which is why they have to wear football helmets and spine pads to protect themselves.

So far this barrel of fun is only big in Montreal, northern Michigan, and parts of England.

DOUBLE-ENDED CARS. Wouldn't it be cool to have a car that went forward and backward *at the same time?* If you'd been around in the early fifties, you could have gotten a double-ended car and done just that.

Auto mechanics welded together the front halves of two same-model cars to come up with each double-ender. With the car fronts facing opposite directions, it was impossible to tell whether the vehicle was coming or going. (Most could only be driven from one driver's seat, but a few way-cool ones were designed to be driven from *either* driver's seat.) Now that's worth a double-take! Now that's worth a double take!

FLYING CARS. *"Up in the sky! It's a bird! It's a plane! It's...a car?"*

Affirmative on those last two guesses. During the last eighty-two years aeronautical engineers have been trying to perfect a vehicle that could be both driven and flown. Between 1918 and 1993, inventors were granted seventy-six patents for "roadable airplanes," also known as "flying cars." There was the 1914 Curtiss Autoplane; the 1946 Fulton Airphibian; the 1959 Aerocar (the nineties model, the Aerocar 1V, is fashioned from a Geo Metro). Other way-cool models were dubbed the CaRnard (its main wings fold over the car when it's on the ground), the Aircar, and the Sky Car.

Now that's what we call a backseat driver!

Sure would help beat that freeway traffic!

If you're dying to catch a glimpse of these double-duty vehicles, head for Oshkosh, Wisconsin. A fly-in of roadable airplanes, put on by the Experimental Aircraft Association, takes place there each year.

HANDWRITING. Convicted felons share more than matching uniforms: their handwriting is eerily similar, too.

Just how does the criminal mind show up in a person's penmanship? Overall, a felon's handwriting is extremely hard to read. The letters slant in all different directions in a single word. The size of the letters varies from letter to letter; big letters pop up next to small letters. The margins are often missing—especially on the *left* side of the paper. The letter strokes look like they were "slashed" on the page. Real letters are mixed with weird, made-up letter shapes. And doodles and strange hieroglyphics show up on important papers.

Maybe police officers ought to start asking the bad boys they pick up to give them handwriting samples along with their fingerprints.

Wha^x do ya mEan, I Xxrite like a crook??

HURLING. If you like to throw things, hurling could be the hobby for you.

Hurling's heyday was the Middle Ages. Back then, people bombed each other by catapulting dead mules and men over castle walls! They did it then pretty much the way they do it now, with a catapultlike device called a *trebuchet* ("treb'-you-shay") that looks like a giant seesaw. The thing you wanted to throw goes at one end; a counterweight goes at the other. When the weight drops...*tally ho!* The projectile is airborne!

In 1993, the International Hurling Society ("dedicated to the art, science, and history of throwing things") was launched. Last year members of the IHS built the world's largest trebuchet, a 100-foot-tall contraption that uses a 55,000-pound counterweight to toss stuff down a 60-by-1,200-foot firing range toward two plywood targets. It can toss a Buick one thousand feet and sixteen-pound bowling balls farther than a football field. Hurl on!

Whew!

Whew!
We thought
you meant
that other
hurling!

Q: You're the country's

best known insect eater in addition to being a retired entomology professor and the former editor of *The Food Insects Newsletter*. If anyone's eaten a lot of insect legs, it's you. What's the ultimate all-bug meal you ever ate?

A: "In May of 1992 the New York Entomological Society gave a famous banquet to celebrate its 100th Anniversary; I was the guest speaker. What was on the menu? Things like mealworm dip. Waxworm fritters with plum sauce. Roasted Australian grubs. Sauteed Thai water bugs. Cricket breads with butter. Chocolate cricket torte. Live honeypot ants. And insect sugar cookies!"

Q: Wow! Tell me what a couple of these dishes taste like?

A: "Ants taste like sesame seeds or rice crispies. Waxworms, which are the larvae of a little moth, are best when deep fried; they have the flavor of bacon."

Q: There's a proper way to eat most foods. Is there a proper way to eat an insect?

A: "If the insect is hard-shelled, you peel off its wings first and then peel off its legs. If you're eating a great big beetle, you might take off the hard shell first so that what you have left is like a shrimp. If it's soft-bodied, you cook it whatever way you want to and eat it. In Africa, people will pluck a termite from a termite mound and just pop it live in their mouth."

Q: Where else is bug eating really big?

A: "Americans think eating insects is Bushmanlike behavior, but it's very common in a lot of nonEuropean countries. Thailand is a big insect-eating country. In Mexico, for example, four hundred different insects are eaten. The menus in some of the best restaurants in Mexico offer *escamoles*, an ant-larve dish that costs about twenty-five dollars for a side helping. In Papua New Guinea, walking sticks are eaten."

Q: Do you ever have a little fun with the fact that you eat insects, like, secretly take a toasted-insect appetizer to a potluck dinner?

A: "No, I've never pulled a prank like that. But people kid me about it a lot. They'll say, 'Hey, did *you* have anything to do with preparing this lunch?'"

INSECT EATING. What would it take for you to chomp into an earthworm patty? Munch on a fried mealworm ball? Taste a two-inch-long toasted Thai water bug?

If your answer is "a gun to my head!" then you're definitely not a natural-born bug eater, or *entomophagist.* But here's what's weird: eighty percent of the world's population *do* dine on bee larvae, caterpillars, grubs, termites, ants, grasshoppers, and crickets! Sometimes the insects are eaten raw, but usually they're roasted, fried, or boiled before they're served. As a source of nutrition, bugs are hard to beat. They provide protein, fat, vitamins, and minerals—for poor and rich alike. Even royalty. The late Emperor Hirohito of Japan, for instance, loved to eat cooked wasps mixed with rice.

So what do insects taste like? Well, fried grasshoppers taste like sunflower seeds. Barbecued tarantulas taste like shrimp. Termites taste like fish. Palm grubs taste like pork sausages. Thai water bugs taste like lettuce. Don't be too smug about never grossing yourself out by eating bugs. Odds are you're already eating some! The Food and Drug Administration allows as many as 225 "insect fragments" per 100 grams of spaghetti. Now *that's* gross!

"A bugburger with cheese, please!"

"No problem. How 'bout some grasshopper fries with that?"

gross! gross! gross!

JIM SMITH SOCIETY. If your name is Jim Smith, there's a club that wants you to join, no questions asked.

The Jim Smith Society is made up of about 1,700 men who share the same name. They have a quarterly newsletter, and for the last twenty-five years, the Jims have met once a year in a different part of the country to visit, golf, play softball, and play Jimgo (Bingo with a twist). So many Jim Smiths in the same room call for calling each other by anything *but* their real names. That's why "Jim" becomes everybody's last name and each man's hometown becomes his first name ("Battle Creek Jim," "Portland Jim," etc.). Talk about a name game!

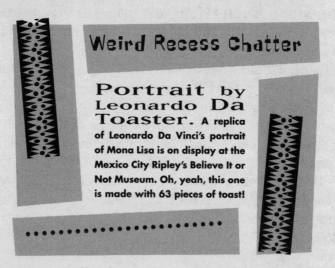

Weird Recess Chatter

Portrait by Leonardo Da Toaster. A replica of Leonardo Da Vinci's portrait of Mona Lisa is on display at the Mexico City Ripley's Believe It or Not Museum. Oh, yeah, this one is made with 63 pieces of toast!

KLINGON. *"TlhIngan Hol Dajatlh'a'?"*

If you're a *Star Trek* fan, you just might answer that question ("Do you speak Klingon?") with a *"HIja', HISlaH"* ("Yes!"). Klingon is the alien language that the same-named warrior tribe speaks in the *Star Trek* TV shows and movies. What's weird is that people are studying, speaking, and becoming fluent in this fictional tongue.

Thanks to *The Klingon Dictionary* (more than 250,000 copies have been sold) and *Conversational Klingon* (50,000 copies of the audiotape have been purchased), Klingon is probably the fastest growing language in the galaxy. And that's not counting all the people who log onto the various Klingon forums on the Internet, or the Klingon speakers on all seven continents who subscribe to *HolQeD* (*Linguistics*), the quarterly journal published by the Klingon Language Institute. How *Huj* ("strange")!

LAWS. Okay, so maybe some laws—like wearing a seat belt—do people some good. But some laws are just plain goofy.

Take the Baltimore law, for instance, that makes it illegal to take a lion to the movies. What were our lawmakers thinking when they proposed such preposterous laws? A lot of these wacky laws were tacked on to real bills that a legislator wanted to defeat as far back as the 1800s. When the bill passed, the loony law did, too. Here are ten of the thousands of ridiculous laws that are still on the books.

- In Hartford, Connecticut, it's against the law to walk on your hands when you cross the street.
- In Gary, Indiana, it's against the law to go to a movie theater within four hours of eating garlic.
- In Chicago, it's against the law for ugly people to walk the streets.
- In Zion, Illinois, it's illegal to give a lighted cigar to your pet.
- In Normal, Illinois, it's against the law to make faces at dogs.
- In Urbana, Illinois, it's against the law for monsters to enter city limits.
- In Kentucky, the law says you absolutely, positively must bathe at least once a year!
- In Kentucky, it's against the law to carry ice cream cones in your pocket.
- In Waterloo, Nebraska, it's against the law for barbers to eat onions between 7 A.M. and 7 P.M.
- In Oklahoma, it's against the law to get a fish drunk.

Too bad there aren't any laws
AGAINST homework!

LIPOGRAM. Could you write a sentence without using the letter *B*? (I just did.) How a*b*out (oops!) an entire book? If you did, you would be the proud writer of a lipogram, a book that purposely leaves out one specific letter of the alphabet.

Nobody knows why writers go ga-ga over lipograms, but they've been churning them out ever since 500 B.C. That's when one Greek writer retold *The Odyssey* in twenty-six volumes, the first volume without the letter "a," the second minus the letter "b," and so on. In the 1700s, German poet Gottlob Burmann wrote 130 poems that were "r"-less (he also refused to say any word that had the letter "r," including his own last name!). In 1939, American musician Ernest Wright published a 50,000-word, "e"-less novel called *Gadsby.* French author Georges Perec just wrote the latest "e"-less novel called *A Void.* Way to go, *G org s!*

Weird Recess Chatter

"One bucket of ant abdomens, please!" In Bogotá, the capital of Colombia, when you go to the movies you snack on something tastier than popcorn: roasted ant abdomens! Yum!

MAIL DELIVERY. These days, most mail carriers zip around in those little white vehicles that look like a cross between a golf cart and a jeep. But before it latched on to its current mail-moving vehicle, the Post Office experimented with some pretty weird ways of transporting the mail. Not all of the mail movers had wheels. Some had paws and hoofs!

Take the Post Office's answer to delivering mail to the southwestern desert in the mid-1800s: by *camel!* Too bad the mail carriers got motion sick from the camel's stride and that the camels often bit, kicked, and—*bleah!*—spat on the riders. In Alaska, *reindeer* were used to run the mail across miles and miles of frozen land. There was just one problem with this Reindeer Express: the reindeer loved to bite the riders. The Post Office switched to dog teams in the 1960s. In the Grand Canyon, a *mule train* still delivers the mail five days a week to the Havasupai Indian reservation located 2,400 feet below the canyon's south rim.

> So *that's* why the price of stamps keeps going up...

MANDATORY ARCHERY PRACTICE. *Ready, aim, release!* If you were a kid during the Middle Ages, you definitely would've become an amazing marksman. It was the law!

From about 800 to 1500 A.D., English law decreed that every man and boy own an archery bow and practice target shooting every day. The goal? To hit human-sized targets from both 100 and 200 yards away—the typical battle ranges of the day.

Weird Recess Chatter

"I'd like to mail this coconut class, please!" You can send a coconut through the mail without wrapping it up in brown paper or putting it in a box.

MESSAGE SENDING. Getting a message to someone can be as simple as typing an E-mail message into a computer and zapping it across the miles. But corresponding wasn't always so easy.

Take the sixth century B.C. Back then, a FedEx sort of system *did* exist, but it was hardly an overnight one. If you had your own empire, like Cyrus the Great did, you sent your special delivery messages by slave. No surprise there. The weird part is that the slave didn't carry the message; he *wore* it.

First the messenger's head was shaved. Then the message was written on the now-bald man's noggin. After the messenger's hair grew back, he was sent off to deliver the message. How to read a message hidden by hair? You got it! The poor slave's head was once again shaved to reveal the secret message.

It's a good thing Cyrus didn't **use Braille.**

the Weird list:

WEIRD WAY TO SEE THE USA

Most people like to travel by plane, train, or automobile. Then there are those who like to get to where they need to go by wackier means. Like, walking backward or somersaulting to their destination. Take a look at this handful of weird road trips:

- In 1931, Plennie Wingo took a year to *walk backward* from Santa Monica, California, to Istanbul, Turkey. (He crossed the Atlantic by boat.)
- In 1980, Joe Bowen *walked on stilts* 3,008 miles from Los Angeles to Kentucky.
- In 1986, Ashrita Furman *somersaulted* from Charlestown to Lexington, Massachusetts (he'd previously pogo-sticked up Mount Fuji). It took 8,341 somersaults to cross the twelve-mile route through the Commonwealth!
- In 1986, Ben Garcia *rode a lawn mower* from Maine to California, a trip that took him two months.
- For two weeks in 1989, Peter Del Masto *dribbled a basketball* nicknamed Old Betsy across Massachusetts (he only lost control of the ball four times!).

MYSTERY SHOPPER. Most people like to eat at fast-food restaurants a couple of times a week, but could you eat at one, say, twelve times *a day?* You'd have to if you were a "mystery shopper."

This weird job requires that you anonymously visit as many as fifteen fast-food restaurants per day. A fast-food spy's mission? To make sure restaurants such as Kentucky Fried Chicken, Taco Bell, and Wendy's have counter help that's friendly and fast, and food that's *exactly* the temperature it should be.

Tools of the trade include disguises (sunglasses or construction worker garb so the counter help doesn't recognize their rater), extra clothes (so ketchup and cole slaw spills don't blow your cover), thermometers (to make sure, for example, that KFC biscuits are 139 degrees when served), and sharp eyes to make sure windows are clean and employee nametags are readable.

So if you see a customer secretly sizing up a fast-food joint, lower your voice and ask him if he's a...shopper. A mystery shopper.

OCTOPUSH. Puck. Gloves. Sticks. Goal. (If you think you already know what sport this gear would prepare you for, read on!) Diving mask. Swim fins. Snorkel.

Snorkel? Yeah, if you guessed hockey, you were *half* right. Octopush is *underwater* hockey! Here's the lowdown on the sport. There are six players on each octopush team (their sticks and swimming caps are color-coded to keep teammates straight). The object of the game is to take a stick and push a brass puck into the other team's six-inch-high by four-foot-long goal.

Octopushers play in a swimming pool that's at least twelve feet deep, and that's ideally thirty-six feet wide and seventy-five feet long.

Octopush started in Great Britain about forty years ago as a way for divers to stay fit during the winter. The game is now played in forty cities and eleven foreign countries!

the Weird

list

LOST AND FOUND

You'd expect people to lose their umbrellas or eyeglasses when they travel by plane, train, or city bus. But how does something like a wheelchair get left behind!? Take a look at some of the weird stuff that frequently ends up in the lost and found departments at mass transit headquarters worldwide:

Wheelchairs
Baby strollers
Bicycles
Artificial legs
Artificial hands
Small dogs
False teeth
Live rats and mice in cages
Urns that hold the cremated remains of the dead

ODOR-EATERS INTERNATIONAL ROTTEN SNEAKER CONTEST. P.U.! If you think kids would be too embarrassed or too cool to enter this competition, think again. Every year about 500 kids aged five to eighteen try to become the kid with the world's smelliest sneakers.

The twenty-one-year-old competition starts with regional competitions in Massachusetts, Alaska, New Mexico, Florida, Texas, and Vermont. Internationally, regionals have been held in Amsterdam, Scotland, England, Japan, and Israel. The kids whose gym shoes rate the "Best of the Worst" in each region are flown to Montpelier, Vermont, where Odor-Eaters are manufactured, for the final nose-hair-singeing event.

And this ain't no foolin' around! Each shoe is judged in eight categories: heels, toes, soles, tongues, overall condition, odor, laces or Velcro, and eyelets. The unlucky judges have included the inventor of Odor-Eaters, a basketball coach, and K-9 Max, a German shepherd trained for police work. Winners receive a $500 U.S. Savings Bond, a new pair of sneakers, a three-and-a-half-foot-tall trophy with a victory symbol on top, and a year's supply of Odor-Eaters products.

What they don't get to keep is their shoes!

Those end up in the Odor-Eaters Hall of Fumes, a beautiful glass-windowed, wooden case that displays six to eight pairs of PU-ed-out shoes on special pedestals complete with plaques that list each rotten sneaker winner's name, hometown, and age. Now that's something weird for the résumé: 1997 WINNER OF THE ODOR-EATERS INTERNATIONAL ROTTEN SNEAKER CONTEST.

ODOR JUDGE. How would you like to whiff mildewed carpets for a living? Bury your nostrils in pitted-out armpits? Smell doo-dooed up diapers? If you were an odor judge, you'd have to rate all those fumes—and more!

To judge an underarm, for example, an odor judge cups her hand to the side of her face, sniffs twice on each side, then assigns a rating from one (not stinky) to ten (*stand back!*). Testing a new mouthwash means analyzing "morning mouth"; rating a new deodorant means sniffing pits. No, we don't want to think about how odorless underwear was developed!

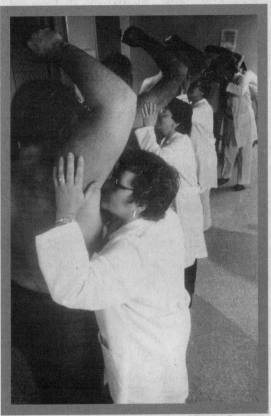

LOUIS PSIHOYOS, CONTACT PRESS IMAGES

OXYGEN BARS. *"The guy in the back needs thirty minutes of oxygen, as soon as possible."* Sound like a doctor ordering treatment for a patient? If you were in Beijing, China, it just might be a line you'd overhear in a bar. As in an "oxygen bar."

The capital of China is so polluted that office workers wanting to unwind after a hard day are willing to pay for what most Americans take for granted: fresh air. Customers tap into the O_2 by sticking the oxygen dispenser's plastic tubes up their nose and inhaling. But heading for the nearest oxygen bar on a daily basis could clear your pocketbook as well as your head; it costs as much as $12 an hour to inhale the odorless, tasteless, and colorless element! Herbal or spice-laced oxygen costs more.

PET TAXI. *Beep, beep!* "Hey, Muffy, hurry up and grab your bone—your ride's here!"

The four-legged finally have a way to get around Manhattan without walking: their owners can call Pet Taxi. This two-minivan service is decked out with a large cage and artificial turf for the comfort of its passengers. Most fares are what you'd expect: cats, dogs, fish. But a few have definitely been on the wilder side—such as a 150-pound turtle and baby sharks. Passengers typically end up at the groomer's, the kennel, the animal hospital, or the airport. Cool way to go, guys!

SCHOOL RULES. If you think *your* teachers are weird when it comes to rules and regs, read on.

If you were a middle school student in Japan, you would be following some rules that are downright bizarre. Your shoes would have no more than twelve shoestring holes. Your shirt would have to have a certain number of buttons. Ditto with the tucks in your shirt. You would have to wear your book bag strap over your *right* shoulder in the morning; over your *left* shoulder in the afternoon. If you wanted your teacher to call on you, you would have to raise your arm forward and at *the exact angle* stated in your school handbook.

The uniform and classroom rules weirded us out so much we were afraid to ask about pit-stop regulations!

Weird Recess Chatter

Color by number.

Two billion Crayola crayons are produced annually.

SECRET LANGUAGES. You don't have to infiltrate the CIA in order to learn a language that only you and your best friend can understand.

Some kids in England, for example, know how to talk in *"back slang."* To try it, spell a word backward in your head, then say that word out loud. "Now that's weird!," would be, "Won staht driew!"

Pig Latin is another way to mask what you're saying. (No, there's no oinking involved!) Here's what you do. Take the first letter of the word you're going to say, put it at the end of the word (unless the word begins with a, e, i, o, or u), and then add "ay." Saying, "Now that's weird!" in Pig Latin would come out "ownay hatstay eirdway!"

Oolcay!

Weird Recess Chatter

Don't **let** this **wig** you out. Wigs were so popular during Roman times that sculptors who carved busts (statues of people from the chest up) went ahead and sculpted several different marble wigs that could be plopped on top of the bust's head as hairstyles changed. "Caesar, let's put the Mohawk wig on Great Uncle Marcus today!"

SILBO. If you ever visit the Spanish-speaking island of Gomera in the Canary Islands, don't absentmindedly whistle. In Gomera, some natives "speak" Silbo, a language that's whistled.

As beautiful as Silbo may sound, it was born from tragedy. In about 100 A.D., what is now Africa was a Roman province called Mauretania. Supposedly, the Mauretanians thought they were being way overtaxed and rebelled. They rioted, then killed the president and governors of Mauretania. A Roman army was sent to Mauretania, where the leaders of the revolt were executed and the rest of the tribe—*ouch!*—had their tongues cut out as punishment! (Ancient Romans didn't mess around.) The tribe was loaded onto ships with some grain and cattle, and banished to Gomera, then the most-western point of the known world.

Since then explorers and world travelers alike have noted the weird way some Gomerans communicate. They stick their fingers in their mouth and, well, warble like a bird. By whistling instead of speaking, Gomerans can communicate with someone as far as five miles away (the gorge-laced island is only eleven miles across). A doctor once whistled ahead to the next village so that when he arrived, sick people were already gathered for treatment. Warble on!

SNOWLESS DOGSLED RACE. What's wrong with this dogsled racing lineup? Fifteen mushers. Fifteen carts outfitted with balloon tires. More than sixty Malamutes, Siberian huskies, and Alaskan huskies. A forty-seven-mile course.

Whoa! Carts with balloon tires? Where's the snow?

the Weird list

MOVIE SOUND EFFECTS

The noise on screen	*How Hollywood does it*
A robber gets punched	Thumps a defrosting chicken with a baseball bat
A doctor performs surgery	Squishes the pulp of a cantaloupe cut in half
A baseball breaks a window	Drops a few lightbulbs on the floor
A kid rips his T-shirt on a nail	Pulls apart two strips of Velcro
A fire crackles	Scrapes one pine cone against another

Not here. Not in March, when this race takes place. The Oregon Dune Mushers Mail Run is the world's longest *dry-run* dogsled race. Huskies pull carts with four wheels over sand along the Oregon Coast. Now that's *doggone* weird!

It's mush, mush—without the slush!

TOMBSTONES. Angels. Crosses. Praying hands. That's what you'd *expect* to appear atop the rectangular slab of marble that identifies a person's final resting place. But not always.

Some people want to stand out even after they're laid to rest; they opt for tombstones in weird shapes. A huge stone baseball, for example, marks the grave of

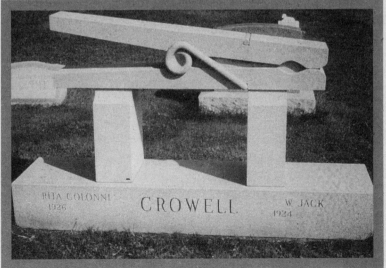

RITA COLONNI
1926

CROWELL

W. JACK
1924

CLYDE A. CHAMBERLIN

William Hulbert, the first president of the National Baseball League. A TV-shaped monument tops the grave of a television producer who's buried in Colma, California. An enormous stone Coke bottle identifies the burial site of a soft-drink lover in Georgia. A giant Scrabble board tombstone spells out (both horizontally *and* vertically, of course) the late Helen Cornelius Bowden's name, occupation, and hobbies. A life-sized Mercedes made of stone marks another grave.

The weirdest tombstone might just be the one created for a still-living clothespin manufacturer. It's a stone replica of one of those old-timey wooden clothespins, complete with a granite "wire" to keep it shut. Now *that's* a headstone that will make any cemetery-goer snap to attention.

Glossary

Abdomen: the hindmost section of the body of an insect.

Aborigines: people who've lived in a land from the earliest time, before the arrival of invaders or colonists.

Acclimatization: the process of getting used to a new climate or surroundings.

Albino: a person or animal with no color pigment in the skin and hair (which are white) and in the eyes (which are pink).

Amnesia: the loss of memory.

Amphibious: living or operating on both the land and water.

Anesthesiologist: a person who gives a medicine that makes one lose sensation or consciousness.

Angler: a person who fishes.

Bangladesh: a country in southeast Asia, east of India.

Canary Islands: a group of islands in the Atlantic Ocean positioned off the northwest coast of Africa.

Convalesce: to regain health after illness.

Cowlick: a lock of hair that sticks up.

Curator: the person in charge of a museum.

DNA: deoxyribonucleic acid, a substance in the chromosomes that stores genetic information.

Embalmed: to preserve (a corpse) from decay by using spices or chemicals.

Entomology: the scientific study of insects.

ESP: Extrasensory perception. Mind-reading is an example of ESP.

Gecko: a house lizard in warm climates, able to climb walls with sticky pads on its toes.

Geologist: an expert in the study of rocks and the Earth's crust.

Geyser: an underground natural spring that shoots a

column of hot water or steam.

Larva: an insect in its first stage of life after coming out of the egg.

Linguist: a student of languages.

Malamute: an Eskimo dog.

Mastiff: a large strong dog with droopy ears.

Mecca: a place that a person or people with certain interests are eager to visit. Named after Islam's holy pilgrimage site.

Mogul: an important or influential person.

Monastery: a building in which monks live as a secluded community under religious vows.

Muumuu: a loose, brightly colored dress.

Parasite: an animal or plant that lives on or in another and draws its nourishment from its host.

Polydactylism: the condition of having an abnormal number of fingers or toes.

Preposterous: absurd, outrageous, crazy.

Psychologist: an expert on the study of the mind and how it works.

Puffin: a black seabird with a short striped bill, somewhat like a penguin.

Reigning: ruling as a king or queen.

Sanitarium: an establishment for the treatment of the chronically ill.

Stalactite: a deposit of calcium hanging like an icicle or a fang from the roof of a cave.

Stalagmite: a deposit of calcium that stands on the floor of the cave like a pillar.

Stethoscope: an instrument for listening to sound in the body.

Tagger: a graffiti artist.

TB: tuberculosis, an infectious wasting disease which affects various parts of the body, especially the lungs.

Tectonic plates: large rock plates deep in the earth that cause earthquakes when they shift.

Udder: the gland on a cow where milk comes from.

Viscount: a nobleman ranking between earl and baron.

Vortex: a whirling mass of water or air, a whirlpool or windpool.

Walking Stick: an insect that is thin and long and resembles a twig.

Winnipeg: a city in Ontario, Canada.

About the Author

Sheila De La Rosa is a writer and editor who keeps extensive files on weird stuff! She grew up in the Midwest, in a pretty normal family except for this: their idea of fun was taking factory tours, and seeing who could first add up the numbers that were stenciled on the side of railcars whenever the family car got stopped by a train ("Twenty-six!" . . . "Thirty-one!" . . . "Sixteen!")

Sheila graduated from the University of Missouri's School of Journalism. She writes books and articles for magazines (she's the "Weird Yet True" columnist for *Disney Adventures*) from her home in Portland, Oregon, where she tools around on a canary-yellow Motobecane Mixte bicycle dating back to the disco days.

What's the weirdest fact you've ever heard? Sheila wants to know!

You can E-mail her at
WEIRD1@teleport.com

or write her care of
The Encyclopedia of Weird
P.O. Box 531
Portland, OR 97282.